Torches

Torches of Joy

John Dekker

with Lois Neely

Crossway Books • Westchester, Illinois
A Division of Good News Publishers

Torches of Joy. Copyright © 1985 by John Dekker. Published by Crossway Books, a division of Good News Publishers, Westchester, Illinois 60153.

Front cover illustration by Dwight Walles

First printing, 1985

Printed in the United States of America

Library of Congress Catalog Card Number 84-72007

ISBN 0-89107-339-6

Contents

Foreword

The Dani people of Irian Jaya on the island of New Guinea are one of the most amazing tribal groups found anywhere on earth. Probably no other tribal people in history have embraced so much change with such great enthusiasm in so short a time. But rapid change, as almost everyone in the world today is discovering, entails risk. And when 150,000 people hurdle from the Stone Age into the twentieth century in one generation, the possibility exists that their society will suffer enormous—and perhaps fatal—disruption. At least eighty-eight tribal peoples have become extinct thus far in this century. Hundreds of other groups languish in cultural limbos, disoriented and oppressed.

The Dani people, though they still face many adjustments, appear to have cleared at least the main hurdle and hit the ground running.

Why the difference?

People like John and Helen Dekker are a major part of the answer. They went to the Dani as missionaries for the gospel of Jesus Christ, but learned also to serve the Dani people as ombudsmen. They helped the Dani discover the Creator who is also their Redeemer. They also helped them find their destiny as helpers of other tribes.

Such a mission naturally required the Dekkers to pass some difficult tests themselves. The story of how they taught the Danis—and learned from them—is an intensely human and readable adventure. It also reflects the spreading influence of two notable Christian institutions.

Prairie Bible College in Alberta, Canada, in addition to training thousands of pastors and Christian laypeople, has also provided approximately 2,500 missionaries, including many who have distinguished themselves notably while serving in a hundred or more nations. John Dekker is a member of that company.

Secondly, John and his wife served under a mission society known as Regions Beyond Missionary Union.

Beginning in 1878, RBMU commissioned its earliest trailblazers to the Congo and later to India. At the turn of the century, it sent Thomas Paine to the Quechuas in Peru. (Paine discovered Machu Picchu, the Lost City of the Incas, in his spare time!) During the 1930s others pioneered in Borneo and, in the 1950s, in Nepal and New Guinea.

It was in this latter field that RBMU placed John and Helen Dekker among the Danis at Kanggime (1960), Stan and Pat Dale among the Yali (1961), Carol and me among the Sawi (1962), Phil and Phyliss Masters among the Kimyal (1964), Costas and Alky Macris among the Lakes Plain people (1967), not to mention dozens of other laborers among these and other tribes.

Currently RBMU International, as it is now called, is developing new fields in the Philippines and Chile.

The saga continues. To learn how this major chapter unfolded, read on . . .

                                        Don Richardson

Introduction

In 1960 the Dani tribespeople in the remote Toli Valley of Irian Jaya (formerly West or Netherlands New Guinea) chose to burn their fetishes, quit their fighting, and listen to God's Word. These were truly Stone-Age people, with only stone tools and no written language. The population of the area was approximately 25,000. They were a hidden people.

Towards the end of 1960, the Regions Beyond Missionary Union (now RBMU International) placed John and Helen Dekker in the outlying Kanggime area. By the middle of the third year (May 1963), more than 100 Danis had been baptized, churches were being established with Dani elders, and the first pastor was ordained. Hundreds more had been taught the Word of God daily. By the fifth year the first Danis had responded to a call to help evangelize another tribe. By the eighth year, the fledgling Dani church sent out missionaries, graduates of its own three-year Bible school.

Today, among the more than 30,000 inhabitants of the Toli Valley there are seventy-nine indigenous churches with more than 13,000 baptized members. These churches are administered by indigenous church councils. Dani Bible schools are taught totally by Dani Christian leaders. Some sixty indigenous missionaries have been sent out to reach the still unreached peoples in approximately twenty different areas of Irian Jaya.

How did this remarkable church growth and maturity come about in such a short time? What was the basic message, and how had it been presented to these totally illiterate, animistic people so they could quickly grasp God's truth and make it their own in such a way that they were able to effectively share it with their fellows, and to plant indigenous churches? What were they taught? How were they sent out? How were the first candidates for baptism chosen and instructed, church leaders appointed, church government decided on? How were the Dani missionaries chosen?

How did they resolve the conflicts between their culture and what they perceived as Christian principles? When false teachers and heresies arose, how did this newborn church deal with them? How did they deal with the incredible hardships and difficulties of the Dani missionaries, and their tendency to impose Dani culture and to be too paternalistic among the churches they now were planting? How did they resolve the clashes between Dani and Western missionaries? Through all of this, what was the changing role of the Western missionary?

It was in Kanggime, Dekker's first pioneer field, that the first baptism in the Toli Valley took place and the first church was established with ordained national pastor and elders. The first area church council was organized here, and some of the first qualified missionaries were sent out by the Kanggime church.

Thus we have chosen to focus on this small area—twenty-three churches with 5,000 believers today—to present it as a model for cross-cultural mission strategy, particularly the discipling of new believers among developing peoples. This chapter from a present-day Book of Acts is truly a chronicle of God's grace and mighty power, and would seem to set a record seldom matched in the annals of modern missions.

Lois Neely

1 Wait and See

Wuninip sat with the other Dani tribesmen in the smoky darkness of the hut. The once bright fire was nearly out, but the men were hardly aware of it as they talked about the new creatures who had entered their world.

"Do you think they are the promised ones who bring us the secret of *nabelan-kabelan* (eternal life) so that once again we can live forever?"

"No, no. They would have to be snakes to bring us that good word, because it was a snake that knew the secret from the first days."

"I think they are cannibals, and that they will eat our babies," a third suggested darkly.

"That cannot be. Did you see how their hearts are joined to the two little ones they call their own? My brothers, it could be that Ndeka is not a spirit, but is a man like us, who takes a woman just as we do, and that she has young as our women do. Yet, his skin is not like our skin. I have seen him rub himself with a white bar and pour water over his body. Perhaps this is what makes his skin white."

"You are all wrong!" Wuninip's brother spat out the words angrily. "They are demons, white demons. We must kill them before they bring trouble to us!"

The mention of demons sent a shudder through the group. Only a week before, Wuninip's brother had been struck by demon spirits and lay dying. Or was it a woman's black magic? They all knew that sickness and death came from one or the other.

The few remaining embers blinked and burned out, as though to confirm the gloominess of the conversation. A hush filled the dark hut as they contemplated the awesome power of the demons.

"What then is to be done with this man Ndeka and the woman and children he brings?" Another Dani impatiently broke the silence. "Are we to kill them?"

"My brothers," Wuninip reasoned, "if we kill them, we will get no more shells, no more steel axes, no more sharp-tasting salt. They may bring us many other wonderful things as well!"

Wuninip's voice reflected his excitement as he continued. "Did you see Ndeka's little box that has very small people inside so that he can talk to others like himself over the hills? Let us wait and see."

"Yes, yes, let us wait, and take every advantage we can, get all we can." On this they had no trouble agreeing.

"We can always kill them later." With this reassuring thought, the meeting broke up.

Wuninip was pleased with the outcome of the meeting. Although he was young, his Dani brothers recognized his ability not only as a warrior, but as a leader. His body was strong, and he carried himself like a leader. He was well-dressed by Dani standards. The net holding his long hair was positioned high on his forehead, with two wild-pig tails on each side of the headband. His arm bands were fashioned from boar genitalia. The long ceremonial gourd was topped with a plume of fur, and his body was greased to a dusky luster. As he walked to his hut, he reviewed the events of the day.

That morning he had watched the white man's steel

bird circle twice and land. A man had stepped out—one he recognized as Ndeka who had come to Kanggime earlier with Kondabaga. Ndeka had stayed only three days that time, while Kondabaga remained and built the dirt strip the great steel bird landed on today. Wuninip remembered how Ndeka had returned to Kanggime later and asked for poles and bark to build a small house. Ndeka had paid him and other Danis with cowrie shells.

They helped me pay for my bride! And he gave me a steel axe after working only two moons. Now I can quickly chop down trees for firewood, and trim poles for fences and houses. With a steel axe—abok! (it's done). And ayee! the salt he gave us! Never have I tasted such salt!

Then his remembrances of Ndeka's earlier visits had been interrupted as he saw a woman with white skin and two little white creatures coming out of the great bird. *Are these our ancestors coming back to life with lighter skin?* He dismissed that idea. *Our people came from a hole in the ground. These have come from the sky.* Ndeka and the woman with white skin were holding the little white creatures. *Could it be that they have children too?*

Being a man of action, he had made his way through the noisy crowd to greet Ndeka and the others—whoever they were.

Now as he lay in his hut, he struggled again with the question, *Why have they come to live among us?*

Sleep didn't come easily.

In a pole house not far away, the white-skinned objects of Dani speculation were spending their first night in Kanggime. Missionaries John and Helen Dekker, with Paul, age sixteen months, and Eva, one month old, had arrived to live among the Danis of the Toli Valley in New Guinea. It was well that they knew nothing of the temporary reprieve from death granted them by the Dani council that night in the smoky hut. Not that John and Helen had never considered the possibility of dying at the hands of this Stone-Age people. They knew that their mission was not without risk.

Settling into their unfinished house, they, like the Danis, had questions and anxieties—only theirs were about the Danis. Even so, they looked ahead expectantly because they were aware of the past—the preparation that had begun in their lives years before. They were convinced that God had led them as individuals and more recently as a couple toward this time and place. They were here by appointment. This knowledge gave them assurance and confidence.

2 The Promise

"It's a boy!" Fien Dekker had heard those words before. John Theodorus Johannes Dekker was the second son of four born to Fien and Remko Dekker. John made his appearance in Holland three days after Christmas, 1929.

Remko Dekker was an importer of fine drapery materials and laces. In early 1931 he moved his business and family from the north of Holland to the Hague. In the city the Dekkers' tall, narrow house was only a five-minute walk from the Peace Palace and a fifteen-minute bicycle ride to the sea, where John and his friends spent much of their time. Each spring they bicycled to a beach to be the first into the still-icy waters of the North Sea. And they were the last to leave the beach in the autumn. A nearby forest was another favorite spot. There the boys built secret hideaways, when they were not raiding those built by other "gangs." John was at the forefront in these spirited battles and in the fights up and down the neighborhood alley where he and his "enemies" pelted each other with chestnuts and pine cones. Known as a tough leader, he sometimes routed the "enemy" with a bold, singlehanded attack. During the winters the boys strapped wooden runners on their boots and skated along the frozen canal at the end of the Dekkers' street.

His friends were heartily welcomed into the Dekker home. Often as many as eight boys sat around the dinner table where John's parents encouraged debate. John's father was well-read and drew out the boys' opinions on topics ranging from theology to bicycle repair. Yet it was a strict home too. When other adults were present in the dining or drawing room, the rule "children are to be seen and not heard" prevailed.

John was a curious child—he had to know how everything worked. This was tolerated until he took apart the family's cuckoo clock and could not get it back together. In spite of some failures, he became increasingly adept at fixing such items as loose doorknobs or squeaky hinges. Outside the home, nature fascinated him. Not content to leave it outside, he filled dresser drawers with dried leaves and assorted dead bugs pinned to cardboard. A terrarium held snakes, lizards, and frogs. Carried away by his curiosity and energy, John was constantly knocking things over in the house. His mother's favorite plants were upset and treasured vases smashed. Whenever anything went wrong, everyone said, "John did it."

At the private church school John also got in one scrape after another. Teachers wearily reprimanded him for talking or not sitting still. His mischievous pranks were well-known and when trouble surfaced, John was blamed for it. Parents and teachers were irritated by this restless youngster. John? He was totally bored. The punishment at school was standing in the corner or outside the classroom. At home, he was sent to his bedroom or to the basement. His father seldom laid a hand on him. No matter what the discipline, or the misunderstanding, or the hurt, his mother encouraged, *"Flink zijn,* John! You must always be brave. Don't cry. You are capable and strong. You can handle this." She was teaching him that Dutch boys and men must always be in control and never show their emotions.

On the sunny morning of May 5, 1940 John heard a roar overhead. Opening the bedroom window, his young heart beat hard as he looked up. Bombers! Dutch fighter planes were intercepting the German aerial attack. Bullets traced across the blue sky. The country was quickly overrun by German soldiers who helped themselves to the food supply. Hollanders soon learned to live on only a fraction of the food they had before. While many starved, John's father was able to trade a warehouse of goods to country people for butter, cheese, and flour. In this way the Dekker family survived.

During the last year of the war little food was left in west Holland. Fourteen-year-old John and other children were stowed into a truck during the night and evacuated to the north country where there were fewer German troops and more food was available. He stayed there with his father's sister until the end of the war.

John returned to the Hague for high school. After he failed three times, his concerned father said, "John, you cannot go ahead with your studies or in business if you do not succeed now with this schooling. You can do it if you want to. I will give you one more chance." John studied until midnight most nights and acquired a taste for learning that never left him. After graduation, he was to prepare to take his place in the family business.

"First we must work on your languages because a great deal of our business is abroad," John's father informed him. Even though John already had taken courses in German, French, and English in school, he was sent to England and France for further studies.

Through the years the strong Reformed faith of his parents had made an impression on him. As far back as he could remember, he had listened to prayers before and after meals. Each morning his mother had read from a daily devotional book, and each evening his father had read from the Scriptures. Sunday was a happy day, when the whole family went together to morning and afternoon worship services. Throughout the week the boys attended young people's meetings and catechism classes, but not Sunday school. "That's for the unevangelized," his father said. From his earliest days John was comforted with the certain knowledge that he was a "covenant child." As a young boy he stood in the church and with joy in his heart looked upward, sure that if he should die, he would go to be with God.

As a young man, he began to feel an emptiness, a lack of purpose in his existence. *There must be more to the Christian life than I am experiencing,* he told himself.

At this time Holland was involved in a war with Indonesia. In September 1949 John was drafted into service with the army. He did not like this intrusion in his life. His new routine meant rising at 4:30 A.M. to march to the shooting range carrying ten rounds of ammunition, only to wait most of the day for a turn to shoot, then hike back. "It's such a waste of time," he complained. "I'd much rather read Shakespeare or Homer and get on with life!"

The war continued, and John's group was scheduled to leave for Indonesia at the end of the year. Then in December a peace treaty was signed, and the barracks began filling with returning soldiers. Even so, after a six-month leave John was required to complete his army training.

"There must be a way to get out of this," he fretted. On leave one weekend, John asked a nurse, "What kind of sickness could I fake that is difficult to diagnose?"

"Brain concussion," she advised and told him the symptoms.

On his next leave John did not go to church for the Sunday afternoon service. Instead, he went to the woods with a friend, and there they concocted a plan. Later that afternoon, when John's parents returned from church, John was in bed.

"He had an accident and hit his head," his friend lied for him. "He's been vomiting and has a terrible headache." Greatly alarmed, his parents called the military doctor. Concussion was the diagnosis. "He must stay home and remain in bed for six weeks. You will have to care for him," the grave doctor told John's worried mother. Mrs. Dekker enjoyed fussing over her boy. John was elated, yet at times felt vaguely guilty as he hid the book he was reading under the pillow and pretended sleep when he heard his mother's footsteps approaching.

When the doctor announced that the patient was able to return to the barracks, John begged off the hard walks and drills. "I've had a concussion; the doctor says I have to take it easy," he lied to his sergeant. The sergeant was not convinced and sent John to be checked by the base psychiatrist. *How will I fake this one?* John worried. After the tests, the psychiatrist handed him a sealed envelope to take back to his captain. John suspected that the contents would expose his deception. Against orders he ripped open the envelope and read the report. It clearly spelled out that nothing was wrong with him and concluded that he was deliberately pretending sickness. He tore up the letter and burned the pieces.

Back at the barracks that evening, the sergeant told him he must report to the captain first thing in the morning. John couldn't sleep. *I've really got myself into a mess. Tomorrow they'll ask me for the letter and I won't have it. I'll surely go to jail for this.* In desperation he prayed, "Lord, I was wrong to do this. I commit myself to you. Please get me out of this, and I promise I'll go right from now on."

Next morning the sergeant was not in sight, and the captain John was to report to had been called away. No one else asked him for the psychiatrist's report. The whole matter blew over, and John thanked God for getting him out of the scrape.

Finally his army service ended, and John returned to France for more language study before joining his father's firm. Though the cosmopolitan Paris scene was exciting, and he enjoyed travel in Switzerland, Germany, Austria, and Italy, inside there was a gnawing. In moments of introspection he acknowledged, *God, I'm a fraud. I deceived my officers. I deceived my own mother. What a liar I am.* His mind searched for a way out of his discontent. *Maybe I should leave home and try something different. I could go to Australia or New Zealand where I have friends.*

When he returned to Holland, he heard that the Reformed church in Canada was flourishing. *Why don't I go to Canada,* he decided. Visas were hard to get, but a Reformed church in Hamilton, Ontario was lining up sponsorship for young people. He applied. Soon word came that he would be sponsored.

Remko Dekker stoically accepted his son's not joining him in the business, but he didn't express his feelings about the decision to John. *Maybe he feels God is leading me to Canada,* John thought. *Or he is hoping I will return to Holland after a while.* John could tell that his mother was finding it difficult to let him go, but she said little. At the waterfront there were some tears, but the Dutch Dekkers showed little emotion—on any occasion.

He arrived in Hamilton in March 1952 and got a job in the shipping department of a textile mill. In the spring he and three other young Hollanders set out to "see Canada" as they headed west to Vancouver for the summer. In the fall they returned to their jobs at the textile mill.

When the next spring came, John and one of his friends, Bob Kempenaar, took off again. "Maybe we will go to the Yukon, or even to South America," they announced. With these dreams and their baggage they set out across the prairies in a pickup truck outfitted with bunks.

Somewhere on the Canadian prairies John realized that nothing had changed. *I am still the aimless, restless person who left Europe. My life continues to lack meaning and direction. I believe God has a destiny for me, but. . .* He tried out his thoughts on Bob.

"What is the point of this running here and there? What are we doing with our lives?"

Bob was not prepared for such heavy questions. He was glad John didn't wait for an answer.

"I believe our lives have to fit in with God's sovereign plan. Another thing bothers me. We know that only through Jesus Christ can a person come into a right relationship with God, yet millions in the world have never heard of him. Why aren't we doing something to let them know?" He wanted answers as he looked at his friend, but Bob had no immediate response. Neither spoke.

John recalled little emphasis in their denomination on a Christian's responsibility to those who had never heard the way of salvation. *In our predestination theology there is no urgency to get out the gospel. "Enjoy your sonship" we were encouraged.* Again he thought about his own life. *But if I were to become a missionary, it would take years of college and seminary.* He forced the matter from his mind.

The idea had a way of returning in the form of memories. John recalled a schoolteacher who often spoke about far-away places where boys and girls had never heard that Jesus loved them. No one had ever suggested that *he* should become involved, but her comments had made an impression on him and came to mind with increasing regularity during the long trip.

After he and Bob arrived in Vancouver, they took a trip to the northern part of British Columbia. Along the way Bob wanted to look at the map and asked John to hold the steering wheel. From his position on the passenger side, John miscalculated a turn and the truck went out of control. There was a spinning through space, a landing in a lake alongside the highway, and then quiet.

"Bob, are you hurt?" Even as John asked, he was trying to test his own capabilities. Though he could move his limbs, he realized he was upside down!

"I—I think I'm all right." Bob also struggled for an upright position. "The truck's on its side!"

Water was quickly filling the cab.

"We've got to get out fast!"

They struggled and maneuvered their way through the windows. Finally they reached shore. Looking at the distance from the highway to the lake, and seeing the partly submerged truck, the exhausted travelers realized the seriousness of the accident. They knew they could have been killed, but for a long time neither spoke as they recovered physically from the ordeal and reflected on what might have been.

"Bob, I feel that our coming through this alive is due only to God's intervention." Bob had no problem agreeing.

They hired a wrecker to pull the truck from the lake, left the water-soaked vehicle at a garage for repair, and returned to Vancouver by bus.

On Vancouver Island they got jobs in a sawmill. Bob soon discovered that a co-worker, Ben Wiebe, was a Christian. After work one day Bob said, "John, you must meet Ben. He feels we all should be involved in getting the gospel to people who have never heard it. What he said reminded me of what you have been talking about."

John arranged a time to talk with Ben.

"How can I prepare for a mission field? If I go to our denominational schools, it will take at least eight years before I could qualify for service. Is there a shorter way?"

Ben suggested Prairie Bible Institute at Three Hills, Alberta. It was a training school he knew well.

John had never heard of a Bible school. He knew only about seminaries.

"With your education, you could be ready for the mission field in three years," Ben continued.

"I have very little money saved," John countered.

Turning to his new acquaintance, Ben made an offer. "John, at this time my children are not following the Lord. If you wish to train for full-time Christian work, I'll pay your first semester at Bible school." John was stunned by the proposal. He promised to pray about it.

Walking back to the bunkhouse, John considered the surprise offer. *He hardly knows me!* "Lord, if this is what you want, I'll go," he prayed. During that prayer he experienced a closeness to God he had not known before. As John indicated his openness to the Bible school proposition, he could hardly contain the great exhilaration he felt. It was as though God had spoken to him! He knew it was what he should do. *This is too good to keep!* Although it was almost midnight, he hurried back to tell Ben.

"I'll go, Ben! I'll take your offer!"

His excitement was so evident that Ben knew John meant it. Ben was surprised—and pleased. "I'll wire the school in the morning to see if they'll accept you right away. There could be a problem getting you in this semester because classes began six weeks ago."

"Lord, if this plan is yours, you will get me into that school," John prayed.

Two days later Ben received word: "Let Dekker come."

John flew to Vancouver and took a train from there to Calgary where he planned to take a bus the remaining eighty miles. At the bus depot he bought his ticket—and a last pack of cigarettes to smoke on the way. Ben had warned him that smoking was not permitted at the institute. As he rode the bus across the prairies, John thought about doing without. He had been a heavy smoker. Arriving at the hamlet of Three Hills, he tossed away the package.

The school truck came by to pick up any students who arrived by bus. John was the only passenger. As they drove to campus Doug Day, the driver, turned and asked, "When were you born again?"

"Born again? What do you mean?"

"When did you become a Christian?"

"I've always been a Christian."

"Come on, John, there must have been a time in your life when you trusted Christ as your personal Savior," Doug persisted.

John was confused. "Doug, I honestly do not know. So far as I know I have always been a Christian. I was baptized as a baby, and that was that."

When they arrived at the school, John went to the registrar's office. "May we see your papers please?"

"I don't have any," John replied. "I just received word to come."

John could see that his was not a typical registration. No references from pastor or employer, and no school transcripts. The registrar began to look incredulous. What were they to do with this confident young Dutchman? They had agreed for him to come, but these problems had not been anticipated. They admitted him.

In his room, John placed his empty pipe on the desk for a paperweight and dug in.

3 Unlikely Pair

The first Sunday morning, Doug Day knocked on John's door. "Would you like to join our prayer meeting?" John had never heard of a prayer meeting, but it sounded like a good idea. He was glad to go along. When the other students knelt to pray, he wondered, *What now?* He had never knelt for prayer, but decided it wouldn't do any harm. Each prayed in turn around the circle, except John. After an uncomfortably long pause, several others prayed and the leader closed.

"I'm sorry, folks, I've been to church, catechism classes, and youth groups, but never to a prayer meeting." John realized he had much to learn, and the students knew they had a maverick in their midst.

In Room 405 on the top floor of the men's dorm, John set about making up the six weeks of the semester he had missed by enrolling late. He had no roommate, but the privacy helped him to better concentrate on his studies. About the only time he took for relaxation was in the shower room where he loved to debate theological issues. Coming from a Dutch Reformed background, he was well-grounded in covenant theology and found it easy to hold his own in discussions with fellow-students who were not familiar with the Reformed tradition.

He studied long hours, mostly in his main textbook—the small black Bible which he had brought from Holland. When summer came, there was no time for leisure. He returned to work in the sawmill.

One day he was assigned to put dressing on the long conveyor belt to keep it from slipping around the pulley. He had never done this operation. In his inexperience, he applied the dressing to the ingoing side of the belt instead of on the returning side. The belt grabbed his arm with such force that he was thrown off his feet. The operator slammed the stop lever and rushed to John, expecting to see a mangled arm still caught between the drum and the belt. Instead he saw the arm was free, and only belt burns and bruises were on John's hand.

"I can't believe it! It's impossible!" the operator kept repeating as he looked first at the arm and then at John.

"Your whole arm was caught in there—I saw it!"

To demonstrate what should have happened, the superintendent, who arrived on the scene, placed a 1″ x 3″ board where John's arm had been and started up the conveyor belt. The board splintered like a match stick.

Others who were present said they had seen John's arm drawn into the belt. "It's a miracle!" they said.

Did God save my arm—maybe even my life? John was awed. *Lord, last year you brought me through the truck accident and now through this. You must have something special for me to do. Maybe you can use me in spite of myself.* To John it was a definite sign that God had work for him to do.

He returned to Prairie Bible Institute rejoicing in the certainty that he was fitting into God's plan. *I don't know exactly what the plan is, but I am determined to be ready.* He signed up for a full schedule and took such varied courses as choir, chalk drawing, tropical medicine, and storytelling. *I will take every course the Institute offers before I graduate!*

The sovereignty of God had been emphasized in all of his childhood teaching. Now it was becoming increasingly meaningful to him. He believed that God was in charge of his life and that as he yielded himself, God would reveal his good plan. More and more he recognized God as King of his life.

During the fall semester of 1955 Ebeneezer Vine, a missionary statesman and veteran of many years with Regions Beyond Missionary Union (RBMU),[1] challenged students with the mission's newest frontier—the Stone-Age Dani people of New Guinea. For centuries these people had been hidden away behind jagged mountains in the interior of the South Pacific's biggest island located just north of Australia. John listened intently as Vine told of a meeting fifteen years earlier with Paul Gesswein, a young American who had served with the United States forces in Papua, New Guinea. Gesswein had told Vine how a military plane had been missing over the island's interior, and as the American pilots searched for it, they were amazed to find valley after valley dotted with villages and extensive garden areas. The military search team found the downed plane with three survivors in the treacherous Wolo Pass. Twelve paratroopers were dropped, and it took them almost a month to get out the survivors.

"It was this rescue party," Vine explained, "which discovered a Stone-Age people totally untouched by civilization."

Vine told the students how Gesswein followed the story closely, and decided that he wanted to go to these people with the gospel.

"After the war Gesswein enrolled here at Prairie Bible Institute. When I addressed the students at that time he asked, 'Mr. Vine, will your mission help me take the gospel to these people?' After careful consideration RBMU accepted the challenge."

Now Ebeneezer Vine was back at PBI, challenging students with the new venture. "In addition to the work of our mission, several others have responded to the call," Vine told the students. "The Unevangelized Fields Mission (UFM) is penetrating the area.[2] The Christian and Missionary Alliance

(C & MA) already has a post in the Baliem Valley,[3] on the other side of the mountain ranges and to the southeast of the Toli River area where our mission is setting up a base. The Australian Baptist Missionary Society (ABMS) is establishing a base in the Northern Baliem Valley, one or two days trek southwest of the Toli area.

"The Dutch, who administered the west end of New Guinea, previously discouraged all mission efforts. They said that it is far too dangerous, that they cannot provide police protection. They warn that these people are fierce cannibals, constantly fighting and killing each other. But finally they have granted permission. Now we need men to go in—men of courage and tenacity, brave men who will do exploits for God!"

Vine's words stirred John. *Is this my call?* He talked further with the mission representative. So did Don Richardson,[4] a classmate.

John wanted to be sure this call was from God. All winter and spring he prayed about it. He also wrote to his parents that the earlier "brain concussion" was a hoax. He confessed the wrongness of the deception and asked forgiveness. In their next letter they acknowledged astonishment, but assured him of their forgiveness.

He decided to go to Holland for the summer. There he continued to ask God to confirm if he was to go to the Dani people of Netherlands New Guinea. While he was home, he again brought up the "brain concussion" episode. He repeated to them his repentance, and his parents reassured him of their forgiveness. By summer's end he knew he should prepare for New Guinea.

If, when John left for Canada the first time, his parents had hoped he might later return to Holland, they knew this time that God was leading him elsewhere. It was a difficult farewell.

When he returned to Canada, he applied to RBMU for

service among the Dani. During his final semester at the Institute, the letter of acceptance came.

The next step toward his goal was language study at Wycliffe Bible Translators' Summer Institute of Linguistics. He hoped to be on his way to New Guinea by Christmas, but realized that might not be possible. *I've got my support to raise, and that could be difficult since I don't know anyone who would back me.* His Christian Reformed church would not be interested because he was not going to the field under its auspices, and he had few acquaintances outside the Bible institute. He planned to go as a single missionary. But then he met Helen.

Helen Clowes had grown up on the Montana prairies where her father was a wheat farmer. Although she was the sixth of seven children, Helen felt lonely, even in school where she was a popular cheerleader. Often she walked alone in the sunset, dreaming.

"Helen, you are a scatterbrained dreamer," her mother chided.

When Helen was fourteen, two summer missionaries held meetings in the small, country schoolhouse. As they sang "What a Friend We Have in Jesus," Helen longed to have Jesus as a friend. That night she prayed that her father would let her go to the summer camp the missionaries announced. It was a "miracle of miracles" to Helen when her father agreed to let her attend. At the camp she professed to be saved, but somehow she had the idea that her salvation depended on her behavior. It was a letdown when she realized later that she was no different.

After graduating from high school, Helen went to Spokane, Washington for nurses training. There a student invited her to a young people's group at the First Baptist Church, and again she met people who reflected the joy of the Lord. In this church for the first time Helen clearly understood that she could not earn her salvation. She learned that though she was a sinner, God loved her. One evening she was led by the Holy Spirit to the altar, where in tears she committed her life to Christ. *Now I can be a missionary,* was her first thought, even though at that time she had no exposure to missions and knew only one missionary.

From the start Helen wanted to know more about the Bible. She read it daily and began to memorize Scripture verses. Meeting with a group of Quakers, she began to learn more about the Holy Spirit and how to listen for his voice.

After her nurses training, while living in a Navigators home, she became engaged to a Christian man, but had no peace. The Holy Spirit spoke to her: "Take off the ring." It was difficult, but she obeyed. "God is the strength of my heart and my portion forever" (Psalm 73:26, NIV), she pledged as she committed herself totally to God. "Lord, I'm completely yours. I'll do as you choose."

After graduation, she got work in Seattle and attended a Brethren assembly where she learned still more about waiting on God for leading. A fear of missionary service was growing within her, yet she was afraid to disobey God. *If I don't do what he wants me to do, he will withdraw blessing from my life, and I'll have nothing.*

She still was certain of the missionary call, but felt inadequate. She was afraid to meet missionaries, thinking they would see through her and recognize that she could never qualify for missionary service. At twenty-two, other matters troubled her too. She worried about being single, about missing out on romance. She wanted to have a Christian husband—a marriage approved by God.

The realities of life interrupted her dreaming. Helen went home to care for her mother who had had a stroke. Another Christian man came into her life. Again she had no assurance that he was the one.

"Twice I've been sidetracked from doing your will by my longing for romance. Today I vow that I will not date anybody for a whole year so that I can concentrate on preparing for the mission field." She put it in her little notebook and added "unless you bring someone into my life so obviously that to not see him would be disobedience."

Soon afterward Helen met Dr. and Mrs. Dick Pitman of Wycliffe Bible Translators, who urged her to attend the Summer Institute of Linguistics in North Dakota where they would be teaching. Helen applied, but Wycliffe wrote back requesting that she go to their program at Briercrest Bible Institute in western Canada.

But I want to go where my new friends are! Helen rebelled. The Lord again gave her what the Quakers call "a check from the Spirit." Before she refused, she prayed. The answer was unmistakable.

"Maybe you'll find a nice young man up there," her mother suggested hopefully. She didn't want her dainty daughter going off to the wilds of a mission field without a man to take care of her.

"No, Mom, I am not going to Briercrest to find a husband. I am going to study." And she set her heart and mind to do just that.

In a class of only seventeen students, it was impossible not to notice the young man with the Dutch accent. After several weeks Helen decided, "He is different!"

John hadn't overlooked the tiny American with the big brown eyes. *She's the prettiest girl in the class.* By the third week, concentrating on his studies was more difficult. *Helen is to be my wife.* Had God impressed this on him? John was confused. He had never dated, yet he had at times daydreamed about a small dark-haired girl—like Helen. Was this just his idea, or was the Lord really speaking to him? *If Helen is to be my wife, God must have spoken to her also,* he reasoned.

Helen was in bed, not yet asleep, when she became aware of the presence of the Lord. "I want John to be your husband." The words were clear. She sat up in bed. "But, Lord, he's such a character!" And then the Presence was gone. Helen was awed that God had spoken about something so special to her.

"Why doesn't he speak to John?" she wondered when two weeks passed and John was not paying any attention to her. The Bible says to "try the spirits," she remembered. So she prayed, "Lord, if this was you speaking to me, please give me one hour alone with John tomorrow." She knew their days were fully scheduled.

That was the day John decided he must get acquainted with Helen. After class he caught up with her and suggested a game of Ping-Pong before lunch. After the game, as they walked to the dining room, he asked, "Could I have one hour with you this afternoon?" Helen was stunned. *One hour— today!* It was exactly what she had prayed for!

That afternoon they walked on the prairies. "Helen, I have been strongly affectioned toward you in my heart," John announced in his Dutch accent. "It has been interfering with my studies. So I asked the Lord if it was not of him, would he please take it away. And if it was of him to give you the same conviction also."

"Oh yes, God told me that you are going to be my husband," Helen replied matter-of-factly. John was dumbfounded. For several moments he continued to chew on a straw, smiling speculatively at Helen.

"In that case, we'd better spend some time together!" he finally concluded.

Students and faculty thought the idea was hilarious and teased them endlessly. "What an unlikely pair," they thought—and said.

"I've never seen two persons more opposite in personality, temperament, and background. You will have many problems," a professor warned. In spite of counsel and clucking, Helen and John remained confident that the Lord had arranged it all.

Following the linguistics course, Helen went to Emmaus Bible School in Chicago for further studies. While there, she had word from RBMU that as John's fiancee she should apply for service overseas. "But I'm not ready!"

"You must apply," they wrote. She did, and was turned down. "I have never seen a more unsuitable candidate," Ebeneezer Vine wrote John.

He is right, Helen thought. *Yet God has called me, and terrified as I am, I will go with the one the Lord wants me to marry. I'll reapply later and leave it with the Lord.*

The following summer, in August 1958, John and Helen were married. During the ceremony Helen was overwhelmed by what God had done. Her heart was filled with love for the man God had set apart for her. "Will you, Helen. . . ?" the minister asked. Choked with emotion, she could only whisper, "I will."

4 Into the Stone Age

The year 1959 was eventful. Helen's answer from RBMU was *yes*. Paul was born in August. John and Helen completed their deputation. Their support was in. Following a final session at the Summer Institute of Linguistics, they were ready to go.

Their outfit was simple: one forty-five gallon drum and one packing case containing dishes, pots and pans, linens and blankets, a few clothes, John's books, and a spring-wound tape recorder.

John was thirty and Helen twenty-six when they left for New Guinea in February 1960. Their first stop on the large island was the hot coastal lowland where they stocked up on food supplies and goods which they could trade with the Danis for work—items such as salt, steel axes, bush knives, and cowrie shells treasured by the interior Danis as currency.

Then a Missionary Aviation Fellowship plane came to take them on the long flight inland to the mission's Karubaga base in the mountains. As the tiny, single-engine plane approached, Helen balked. *I can't take little Paul on that!* Inner resistance and fear tugged away as she slowly approached the plane. But soon she and Paul were strapped into one seat and John into another. For 150 miles they flew over crocodile-infested swamps. *No places to land in case of*. . . Helen looked into Paul's tiny face and held him more tightly.

They flew into mountain ranges 11,000-feet high and, it seemed, never ending. Sometimes the plane climbed higher to fly over a peak. Other times it slipped through the treacherous passes. In one of the ascents Helen cried out, "Why doesn't he turn!" as she saw a mountain directly ahead. The pilot deftly lifted the plane up and over, just as he had planned to do all along.

Helen felt increasingly ill, unaware that she was in the early stages of her second pregnancy. And she was more frightened than she had ever been in her life.

"Helen, you are complete in me," the Lord consoled her.

"Thank you, Jesus," she whispered. "Terrified, but complete."

At last the plane descended to follow the slate gray waters of the Wunin River churning through the Toli Valley. On each side mountains reached skyward beyond the view of the plane's passengers. At a meeting of the Wunin and Konda Rivers the pilot turned left and flew along the Konda toward Karubaga. Still descending, he pushed the throttle forward to reduce speed. Looking below, the Dekkers saw the mission buildings clustered on the Karubaga Plateau. The pilot swung wide to circle the strip. Again a mountain seemed to be right on their course, but the plane straightened for its final approach. Then they were down.

When they stepped from the plane, John moved forward, eagerly shaking hands with the Dani men who crowded around. Helen again tightened her hold on baby Paul as she looked at the throng pressing toward them: Dani warriors, naked except for pubic gourd and glistening boar tusks piercing their noses; women in string skirts. The men's skin was smudged black and greasy; markings were scratched on their faces and upper torsos. They shouted and pushed. The stench of neglected ulcers and the sight of runny eyes and noses accentuated her nausea. Culture shock and fear nearly overwhelmed her as she moved reluctantly forward, through the crowd, to their house.

Inside, Helen hoped to have an interlude in which to recover. Little Paul had been in her arms during the long trip and needed to stretch his legs. Eagerly he crawled on the bark floor while Helen started to unpack. *What was he chewing?* Quickly she reached into his mouth to remove whatever it was. *A cockroach!* Another wave of culture shock.

The Dekkers' assignment to Karubaga was temporary. Earlier Paul Gesswein and Dave Martin had gone to check the possibility of building an airstrip at Kanggime. When it appeared to be feasible, the mission decided that when the airstrip was complete, the Dekkers would set up a base at Kanggime and pioneer in that area. In the meantime they were assigned to language study and medical work at Karubaga.

From the first day there was no lack of sick and wounded needing attention. Helen's first patient arrived during a tropical downpour. He was a chieftain's son who had fallen from a tree and split his lip.

Dear Lord, how can I ever pull together a jagged tear in such soft tissue in this makeshift situation? She stood in mire and watched worms from the grass roof drop all around her. *And it is so dark! I'll have to forget about sterile surroundings and light and get on with the job. Please help me, Lord!*

Gently she stitched the lip. *How can he hold so still?* Then she gave him an injection of penicillin. There were no complications.

Later, after a short time at Karubaga, the tribes of the area were still fighting one another. One day John heard, "Ndeka, Ndeka!" from outside their house. He stepped out and found several Danis carrying a man shot full of arrows. *Not this!*

"Ndeka, will you take out the arrows? If they remain in the flesh they will burrow deeper and deeper. We cannot pull

them out—they are barbed!" They knew—and John knew—
that the flesh had to be cut in order to remove them.

"I have no experience in this. I'm not a surgeon."

They pleaded, "You always help us when we need it!"

John rolled up his sleeves while they pumped up the little kerosene lamp. The newly ordained surgeon froze the area
around the imbedded arrows. He prayed and made the first incision, and then another, carefully, aware of the danger of cutting an artery. One arrow was out. Again he made an incision
as the Great Surgeon directed his hand. Another arrow. Finally all were removed.

In June John accompanied Dave Martin on the twenty-
one-mile trek to Kanggime. After nine hours on the trail, he
saw for the first time the site of his future work. *Kanggime*
("The Place Where I Die")! Its name reminded him of the im-
mensity of the task ahead: to offer life to people steeped in
darkness. His legs were weary from the long trek, but his confidence didn't waver. It was rooted not in himself, but in God
who had called him to this place. "Lord, you will enable and
direct. 'Not by might nor by power, but by my Spirit, says the
Lord'" (Zechariah 4:6, NIV).

John remained in Kanggime three days, getting an
overview of the area and meeting some Danis before returning
to Karubaga to finish building a missionary residence and to do
more language study while Dave stayed to direct the building
of the airstrip. John trekked back to Kanggime six weeks later
with Dave Steiger, an MAF pilot, to see if the strip was ready
for planes to land. After getting the go-ahead, the first plane
arrived with nails and other building materials that were not
available locally. At that time John met Wuninip, bought
poles from him, and hired him to do some of the work on the
storage shed.

John and his helpers completed the 20' x 20' storage
shed. But before construction of the house began, he had to fly
to the coast with Helen to await the birth of their second child.
Helen had contracted amoebic dysentery two weeks after their

arrival in the country, making her pregnancy a trying one. Eva weighed only four and one-half pounds at birth. One month later, in early December of 1960, John and Helen, Paul who was sixteen months old, and Eva were flown into Kanggime.

Settling into their new life in Kanggime was so hectic the Dekkers almost missed Christmas. Lumber and building supplies were still piled in the front room of their unfinished house, and there were no shutters on the windows. In the living room a rough-hewn table, a bench, and two lawnchairs were the only furnishings. The Danis tried to make it up to them with a welcoming feast of sweet potatoes, sweet potato greens, and a fatted pig.

Several days after the event, John was surprised when one of the Dani men came to him and said matter of factly, "Ndeka, I'd like to have a bush knife."

"But you have not worked for it," John answered.

"I gave you a pig," the Dani retorted.

"Wait a minute, I didn't ask you to kill your pig for a feast."

"I gave you a pig, and now I would like a bush knife." The Dani stubbornly stuck to his request.

This "payback" was news to John. "Wuninip, how do I handle this?" he asked his new friend. "You better pay off the man, Ndeka. You see, if you accept a gift, it entitles the giver to demand something he wants in return."

John learned that in the Dani culture the idea was to give in such a way that the other person was obligated to you, sometimes out of all proportion to the original gift. John tried to keep this in mind, but often realized too late that the Danis had taken advantage of him.

Each day forty to fifty Danis gathered on the Dekker porch for medical treatment. They came with tropical ulcers or wounds from wild pigs, with influenza or pneumonia. Little children whose fingers had been cut off as a sign of mourning or to show their ability to endure pain were among the frequent patients. The Dekkers heard how "the expert finger-cutter" moved through the area, recruiting children who resolutely placed their fourth and fifth fingers on a board and looked away while the "finger-cutter" lowered the stone adze and chopped off the fingers at the second joints. The children seldom cried out, but often their fingers became badly infected.

Soon after the Dekkers arrived, a flu epidemic swept through the area, and many developed pneumonia. Pigs were sacrificed to appease the evil spirits, who in the Dani mind had brought on the epidemic. The Dani word for sickness (*kugi andi*) means "evil spirit pain." The Danis believed the spirits made all sickness, and that all death except through war, murder, or accident was due to spirits or witchcraft.

The most heartbreaking cases were the children. Many died because they were repeatedly taken out in the rain. Dani mothers didn't understand that babies were easily chilled in the cold rain and vulnerable to pneumonia. Because the mothers had to take their babies and children with them when they went to the gardens each day to gather sweet potato vines, the babies were exposed to all kinds of weather. Hardly a youngster was free of a runny nose. Often the parents brought the child to Helen when it was too late for medicine to be effective. When they did bring the baby at the beginning of an infection, Helen always warned, "You must be sure to give the baby all the medicine." But often as soon as there was improvement, the parents stopped the treatment and the baby relapsed and died. Helen felt frustrated and heartsick when the parents failed to follow through. Many other children and adults died simply from lack of food, because the witch doctor had told the Danis they should not eat when they are sick.

Some were persuaded that they had been "hit" by witchcraft and would die. And they did, for no apparent physiological reason. The Dekkers recognized that there were illnesses which were caused by demon power. "Pray to Jesus that the medicine will work," Helen encouraged the women. The

power of the evil spirits was strong, and it was not easy for the
Danis to cut themselves off from the old ways, even when they
had seen miraculous recoveries. More than once a relative of a
sick person asked, "Can't we kill just one little piglet to help
God make up his mind to heal the sick?"

"Helen, do you realize we are spending hours in the
medical work each day? We should not be doing anything we
can teach the Danis to do. They're capable of looking after
most of this medical work. Let's see how fast we work ourselves
out of jobs."

At first this was difficult, because they still could not
communicate well. They began by teaching the Dani clinic
helpers to clean the area needing treatment. "This dirt is causing sores," Helen and John explained to the trainees.

"Why are we doing this for the patients?" John asked
one day. "The people can clean themselves before they come."

"Right," Helen agreed. "No bath, no treatment!" This
was a drastic measure for people who never bathed. The
streams were cold, the highland air was chilly, and they had
no way to dry themselves, but they agreed to do it. Helen sent
off an appeal: "Please send towels!"

The clinic helpers learned to swab and dress the yaws—
tropical ulcers that become open sores which often extend two
to three inches, deep down into the flesh, disfiguring large
areas of the body. One little girl with yaws had one buttock
almost gone, and sores on her arms. "She has been afflicted by
the spirits for many moons," her relatives said. "We have
sacrificed a small pig to the spirits, but the sores have not gone
away. She smells very bad. Can you help us?"

After an injection of penicillin, the ulcers dried up
within a week and in another week had completely disappeared. Because yaws were a common problem, Helen taught
the clinic helpers to boil the needles and to give intramuscular
injections to patients.

The Danis also learned to dispense medicine. Since at this point they could not read, the Dekkers used color-coding. John or Helen diagnosed the problem and gave the patient a colored card. If the patient handed the clinic helper a blue card, he matched it to the medicine bottle with a blue tag taped to it. At times the Dani helpers mixed things up and Helen and John got impatient. "No, no, not that way!" they scolded. Then they felt badly that they had been impatient. John got so angry one day that he cuffed one of the young Dani men. He asked the Dani's forgiveness and later gave him a knife. The Dani brought John a chicken, and the rift was healed.

John also taught the clinic helpers to pull teeth. Extracting or giving aspirin were the only ways he could help those suffering with toothache. A dentist in Canada had taught him to use an old pair of forceps. With the Danis' pain tolerance higher than that of most Westerners, John pulled teeth without giving an anesthetic.

On the whole, the clinic helpers learned quickly and were astonishingly skillful at the procedures. Within six months they handled most of the medical work, which consisted mainly of dispensing aspirin, treating sores, and giving injections. The Dekkers diagnosed and cared for only the severe cases. As a result, their clinic time was cut to about one hour a day even though they were treating 1,500 patients each month. The charge for medical treatment was one sweet potato. This "pay" was given to the witness men.

The Dekkers were always desperately short of medicine. "We have so much sickness, we do not have even aspirin anymore. Please send malarial medicine, sulfa, and penicillin, as well as aspirin and other basic drugs," they wrote friends back home. The response was good, but still there never seemed to be enough to meet all the needs.

The bit of midwifery John had picked up along the way was put to the test. He went out on maternity cases rather than

Helen when their children were small. Usually the local mid-wives sent for him when the placenta would not come away. One night when John was visiting in a village a short distance from Kanggime, he was awakened at four o'clock by shouting and knocking on the wall. "Ndeka, a woman has a baby and is in trouble."

"You have your medical workers. That is their business," John responded sleepily.

"They do not know what to do!"

"It's raining and dark, and I just don't think it's necessary for me to come." Dekker had learned more than once that the Danis asked for him when they were capable of handling matters themselves.

"The baby's feet are out, but the rest is not yet born." *A breech birth! The life of the mother could be in danger. I don't know how to deal with this; yet maybe I know more than anyone else.* He quickly dressed.

"How far away is the woman?"

"Just over one little bridge, close by."

The batteries were weak in his little flashlight, and it gave only a faint glow when he held it close to the ground. A hard rain complicated the walk. John could scarcely see. The Danis went ahead to lead the way for what seemed a long distance. "Aren't we there yet?" John asked.

"It's very close," they insisted. On they continued, through the mud and over a rickety, slippery bridge, over fallen tree trunks, through more mud. John wondered what the Danis meant by *close.*

Finally they entered a little home. The wife of a government official was trying to deliver. She was very weak. "Lord, I can't do this," he cried inwardly. At the same time he knew he would have to deliver the baby. Earlier he had witnessed a Dani woman having a breech delivery, and the doctor had explained the technique to him. As he faced the need to duplicate it, he clearly recalled the manipulation the doctor used. He knew the Lord was showing him exactly what to do.

If he had not been there, certainly there would have been serious complications, and most likely the woman would have died.

John got out of most night emergencies by providing a kerosene storm-lamp for the chief clinic helper, who was delighted with the lamp and the job.

In fireside chats and over meals of sweet potatoes in the huts over the mountainside, the Danis talked about the Dekkers' powerful medicine. They liked it almost as much as they liked the steel axes.

5 The Neighbors

Wuninip sat with his wife Warikwe, eating the supper of sweet potatoes and leaves she had prepared. They were at the women's house where she, according to Dani custom, stayed with the children and pigs. The village was Wama, an hour's walk from Kanggime.

Warikwe was glad when Wuninip came to her house or when he surprised her with a visit while she worked in the garden. Earlier Warikwe had been pledged to another who had paid her relatives two of the five pigs agreed on for a bride price. The family had already eaten them when Warikwe announced, "I do not want that man. I want only Wuninip!" And she held her ground through much bickering.

"But how are we to pay back this man when we've already eaten the pigs?" her relatives stormed.

Then Wuninip, the handsome, brave warrior, a leader in his clan, paid Warikwe's parents five pigs, including two to pay back the other man and his relatives. Wuninip and Warikwe were married.

Warikwe was happy to spend her days planting and weeding the large sweet potato gardens Wuninip had cleared, tilled, and fenced for her. After her baby was born, each morning she tenderly placed the little one in the large string bag she had finger-crocheted from strong bark fibers and lined with soft ferns and leaves that snuggled around the baby. She lifted the bag onto her back and looped the straps around her forehead. With digging stick in hand and baby on her back, Warikwe hurried along the trail into the forest, her string skirt swishing gracefully around strong bare legs. As other babies were born, she cared for them the same way. Wuninip was proud of how hard she worked. In the large gardens she grew potatoes to feed the many pigs he purchased. He gave the biggest feasts in the clan.

Now they talked at the close of a day. "Warikwe, what do you think of Ndeka and his woman? Are they ancestral spirits who have come back to us? Or are they white demons who will eat our babies?" She was pleased that he asked.

"At first we women thought Ndeka must be a spirit," Warikwe replied, "because he is so tall and white. But now that we see he has a wife and children, we think they must be real people, like we are. I would like to hold those white babies." She spoke with longing.

"Warikwe," Wuninip continued, "for years we have lived in so much fear. We are afraid of the evil spirits, especially at night. We are afraid of our enemies. So much we have been at war with other clans. We are tired of having to build new houses when ours are burned down—tired of building new fences and planting new gardens when ours are torn up. It is long hard work when we have had only stone tools."

Warikwe agreed. Wuninip went on, "Ten moons ago, the Ilaga Danis from over the hills[1] went to Karubaga. They told the Danis there that if they would stop their fighting and burn their fetishes and bows and arrows and listen to God's words, they could find *nabelan-kabelan* and live forever. They said there is a God who will talk to them, but they could not hear him until they did this.

"You remember that six moons ago we men at Kang-gime decided that we, too, were tired of the bloodshed and wars, of being chased from our villages. After much discussion and deliberation with the clans of this area we agreed to stop our fighting and to burn our fetishes.

"Now I want to listen to *kiwone* (God's talk). Each day Ndeka is telling the people God's talk. I like this man, and he likes me. He wants me to help him make the airstrip longer, and he speaks of little ponds for fish. What these fish are I do not know. He wants us to build a little house where sick people can come for Ndeka's wife's medicine, which he says is stronger than the shaman's.

"Warikwe, I would like to build a house in Kanggime where we could live together, like Ndeka and his wife. Would you like that?"

Warikwe couldn't think of anything she would like more. In the Dekkers' front yard Wuninip built a little rectangular house with flowers around it, just like the Dekkers. Each morning Warikwe walked an hour to her garden and worked all day, while Wuninip helped John and listened to God's words. And Warikwe sometimes held the white babies.

While Warikwe was thrilled with her upgraded living standards, Helen was just coping with the multiple adjustments of her new lifestyle and the debilitating effects of the amoebic dysentery. Their new pole house had some nicer features than the one in Karubaga. John had rigged up a gravity water system with polyethylene piping running from the spring on the mountainside 300 yards from their house. This gave them running water, a bucket shower, and an indoor flush toilet. She was grateful for these improvements, but the rooms tended to be cool and dark. The small windows of opaque plastic let in little light or sun. When it rained, the sound on the aluminum roof was deafening. As Helen looked down the valley toward the distant gorges, she saw only mist-shrouded mountains—not just once in a while, but nearly every day. Located slightly south of the equator with an elevation of 4,500 feet, Kanggime had a perpetual springlike climate; but most afternoons the sunshine gave way to rain or mist. This contributed to a closed-in effect in the dark little house where Helen spent most of her time. *I feel so isolated,* she thought day after day.

Keeping food on the table was a struggle. She was learning to bake bread in the old-fashioned wood stove, but with frequent disasters. Although they had canned meat and cheese from Australia, at this time they had to rely on whatever vegetables and fruit they could buy from the Danis—mostly sour bananas and stringy sweet potatoes. Helen was nursing Eva and was concerned about not having adequate food for the babies. John ordered vegetable seeds and fruit trees in an effort to improve their food supply and quality.

It was impossible to keep the bark floor of the house clean. Consequently little Paul never stayed clean either. When Helen scrubbed the floor, it did not dry well and was damp and cold for days. Dirt and dust tenaciously clung to the webs that the never-tiring spiders spun on the woven bamboo walls. Outside one could hardly avoid stepping in pig or dog manure. The Dani children constantly popped a variety of roasted insects into their mouths, and the adult Danis took food from their mouths and gave it to the children. All this distressed a registered nurse trained in sterile procedures.

Other annoyances made daily life stressful for Helen. Dani youngsters gathered under the Dekker house and created disturbances or broke off flowers. It seemed that every washday socks vanished from the clothesline, usually one of a pair so that soon the family had no matching socks. The Danis treasured these socks, especially the children's little ones, for storing their precious cowrie shells. Towels, too, disappeared from the clothesline. Mostly, Helen could not get used to the Danis continually crowding around her. All the time people were standing on the veranda looking in, pestering her for work. It was wearing her down.

"Helen, you must let the Danis help you. You should not be doing anything a Dani can do. The young boys can gather wood and keep the fires going for you. They can empty slop buckets. Ask someone to peel and cook the potatoes, sweep the floors, and do the laundry for you. This is the only way we'll get to know these people, and they'll get to know us."

Helen prayed that God would direct her to the right person. Then she stepped out onto the porch and asked, "Who would like to work for me?"

"I would," twelve-year-old Leleki responded, and she stepped through their door and into their lives. This lovely young Dani woman turned out to be one of the most beautiful blessings in Helen's missionary experience. Leleki was clever and learned quickly. She had a gentle, happy disposition that endeared her to everyone, and especially the children whom she cared for as her own. All the Dani youngsters fought for a turn to carry the Dekker children on their shoulders. The older people doted on the white babies and liked to touch their soft white skin. It was soon obvious that, perhaps more than anything, the Dekker children were building a bridge to the hearts of the Dani people. And the children thrived on it.

But in March Helen faced a new physical problem. The abdominal pain came suddenly and was severe. At first she thought it might be dysentery, but the pain was steady rather than cramping.

"John, I think it is appendicitis." As a nurse she thought about the other symptoms of appendicitis, especially nausea. She prayed, "Lord, you know how prone to nausea I am. If I start vomiting, the appendix will rupture. Please keep me from nausea. And, Lord, I can bear the pain, but I can't face the fear." Immediately the Lord gave peace—without nausea.

Toward morning the generalized pain lessened and became more localized. Due to the distinct tenderness in the lower right abdomen, she knew it was appendicitis. After consulting by radio with a doctor at a highland station, John and Leleki got Helen's things ready and waited for the plane to take her to the coast hospital. Since Helen was still nursing Eva, they took her with them.

The MAF plane did not arrive until afternoon, and then

the one-engine plane had to fly high through rough weather. On this trip there were no thoughts of crocodiles or mountain peaks, only prayers that they would reach the hospital before the appendix ruptured. At the coast an "ambulance" took her on a forty-five minute drive over a winding jungle road to the Dutch hospital.

"Acute appendicitis," the doctor confirmed as he ordered the patient rushed to surgery. "One more day would have been too late," he told them after the operation. "It would have ruptured."

Back in Kanggime it was soon obvious that Helen had cleared one hurdle only to face another. One leg began to swell. She and John became alarmed when it had swollen to nearly twice normal size and her temperature had risen higher and higher. Again John got on the radio, reporting symptoms to the doctor at the coast. He diagnosed the problems as systemic blood poisoning, but the cause was a mystery. Like a drought time with no clouds in sight, the insidious infection settled in, bringing a high temperature, weakness, and times of delirium. For days Helen's temperature hovered at 104° while John and the mission staff prayed that the antibiotic would counteract the poisoning. Finally, with thanksgiving and relief, they watched the swelling subside and the temperature return to normal.

While John was learning the difficult language, he worked with the Dani men, moving ahead in community development. He was anxious to improve their food supply, but first he got the house more livable for Helen and the babies. He fitted some windows with louvres and completed the septic tank system. Because the Dekker front porch was not adequate for dispensing medicine, a clinic was a must. John began to build a square pole-and-bark structure using poles the Danis brought him. As the building progressed, he couldn't figure out why the job was taking so many poles. "Surely I've bought enough," he insisted to the Danis who presented him with another bundle.

"You have only a few," they informed him. Sure enough, when John checked the pile, there were far fewer poles than he had bought. "What has happened to them all?" John wanted to know. Then someone told him that after he paid them, a few of the Dani were taking poles from the pile at the back of the house, and bringing them to the front and re-selling them to him. He had bought some of the poles two or three times! *Score another for their ingenuity*, John thought as he was again outsmarted.

When the clinic was completed, he got to work on the garden. The earth was so leached by heavy downpours that good topsoil was needed to fill. The Dani women went to their gardens and filled large net leaf-lined bags with black dirt, loaded them on their backs, and returned to the gulley in front of John's house. The men helped set out groves of cultivated bananas to replace the sour, plantainlike variety which the Dani used mostly for cooking. They also planted lemon and orange trees.

John was impatient with gardening and anxious to get on with other work. Like the Dani women, Helen took over while the men went off to work on the airstrip. Although a far-mer's daughter, she didn't know much about growing vegeta-bles, and her garden didn't produce. She called her Dani helpers and gave the seed to them to plant in their own gar-dens. As a result of letting the Danis do it, the Dekkers enjoyed swiss chard, lettuce, tomatoes, and marble-size white pota-toes. *Maybe I should let them plant flowers too*, Helen won-dered as she surveyed the growing vegetables. She and the Danis teamed up and set out red and yellow cana lilies, fuschia, bougainvillea, and multicolored "working lizas" which thrive in wet places. "Why would anyone want to go to all this work for something you cannot eat?" the Danis won-dered among themselves.

For the men, widening and lengthening the airstrip

from 1,200 to 2,000 feet was hard labor. The rocky soil was densely imbedded with large stones and boulders. Some were dislodged by much pushing and shoving, using the Danis' stout, hardwood digging sticks, then rolled off the strip. To move the boulders that would not budge, the Danis excavated underneath and lit a fire. After an hour they dashed cold water on the hot rock and watched it crack into pieces.

They enjoyed hard labor and liked working together, chanting, and shouting. They asked John for work because they wanted the cowrie shells, axes, knives, and salt. On a trip to the coast he had purchased 500 pounds of scrap spring steel from old cars. The Danis were anxious to earn ten-inch strips of this steel. By sharpening one end on a rock and fastening the piece to their original stone adze handle, they had a tool for cutting brush and trees. They could earn one of these pieces of steel with two weeks' work. An axe took a month.

All these activities served as replacement projects for men who had lost their main occupation when they gave up interclan fighting. No longer did they need to spend their days cutting and sharpening arrows and keeping alert for enemy attacks. Except for a little hunting or preparing new gardens, they had little to do. Ndeka offered wonderful treasure in exchange for curious work.

"We will make fishponds," John announced to the work crew. "Fish?" "Ponds?" They had never seen fish because their rivers were too swift and too clogged with mud and silt from landslides for fish to live in. They had no understanding of dams or ponds. John supervised the Danis in digging out five shallow basins approximately forty to fifty feet in diameter, sloping to a five-foot depth at the center. Each pond flowed into the other and was fed by springs on the Kanggime Plateau. "Wuninip, you will be in charge of the ponds. The night temperatures are low enough to keep the water cool."

The project was a great curiosity to the workers. When the plane brought aerated bags of fish for the ponds, Dani interest was high.

"The tilapia will eat the mosquito larvae, and you can eat the Japanese carp," John explained to the excited on-lookers. "The carp will be big enough to eat as soon as you can shoot them with your bow and arrow." When that day came, the Danis eagerly shot the carp, wrapped them in leaves, and placed them in the cooking pit. *Wa! Wa!* The fish became a great favorite and provided protein.

John also brought in leghorn chickens, to improve the nutrition of both the Danis and his own family. These were a novelty. The only large bird the Dani had seen were the *mbeni* bird or wild forest hen and the cassowary bird, but the casso-wary was nearly extinct. The project soon ran into problems because the Danis did not feed the leghorns and they became scrawny. And because the leghorns could not fly into the trees, they often were killed by the ever-hungry village dogs.

We'll have to find chickens that can scratch for them-selves and can fly, John decided. He didn't know the first thing about crossbreeding, but the next time he flew to the coast he bought a Rhode Island Red rooster and several smaller village chickens. The combination proved successful when their off-spring could fly into the trees to escape the dogs and to roost at night. The villagers were delighted with the creatures, but the eggs they brought were not always fresh. To check, Helen placed them in a basin of water. If they were fresh, the eggs sank. Too often they floated.

Elated with his success in crossbreeeding chickens, John brought in better quality boars to upgrade the small, semiwild native pigs. Pigs rated highest in the Dani culture; next came sweet potatoes, and finally the Danis themselves. Pigs were crucial to their economy and society. A man's wealth was measured by his pigs. With pigs a Dani could buy more wives who would grow food which he could sell to buy more pigs. Dani women and children rarely got to eat the pigs, since they were slaughtered mostly for ceremonial feasts or sacrifices in which only men participated.

John looked for another protein source from which the

women could benefit. On the next trip to the coast he brought home two pairs of rabbits. These were prolific, and the Danis found them good eating. So did the dogs, who were trained hunters. "You'll have to choose," John told them. "It's obvious that you can't have both dogs and rabbits." The Danis quickly resolved the dilemma by eating their dogs.

Another area of concern to the Dekkers was the high incidence of tropical ulcers, severe eye infections, parasites, pneumonia, and the high rate of infant mortality soon after birth. John and Helen immediately began to teach the need for sanitation among the villagers. The Danis had already observed that if they drank from water the pigs had been in, they became ill; so they were getting their drinking water from uncontaminated mountain springs, but there were no latrines. It was the Dani custom to simply go a short distance beyond the village into the forest. As a result, pigs and flies got into the feces and spread disease. In each of the villages of the region, John supervised the digging of deep pit toilets which could be covered by a large flat stone.

Mountain trails were extremely hazardous in places, and many Danis had been swept to their death in the swift-flowing rivers after a flimsy low-hanging bridge gave way in flooding. John found it difficult to negotiate the slippery ledges dropping off into deep gorges. "Let's work together to make these trails more safe," John suggested. They widened paths and built solid log bridges, anchored firmly on both banks of the river, to replace the treacherous single logs or swinging pole-and-vine structures.

6 Kiwone

As John and the Danis worked together on various projects, John talked with the men, learning more of their language. He asked questions about their beliefs and drew out their thoughts.

"What is your origin? Where did your forefathers come from?"

"Our forefathers came out of a hole in the ground, far away in the place where the sun comes up."

"What about your women?"

"Some say that when our ancestors came out of the ground, the pigs came out too. The men found a large log lying near the hole, and with their stone axes they split the log open and out jumped the women. Each man grabbed a woman to be his wife, and to look after his pigs and his gardens."

"That is only a *mbynypak* (myth)," an elder Dani scoffed. "The real truth is that everything came up out of the hole—men, pigs, women, dogs, butterflies, everything. When all of these creatures came to a great water, they wondered how they would get across. A large snake was coiled nearby. 'I'll help you,' the snake offered. He uncoiled his long body and arched it over the water for all to walk across. That is how we came to this place."

"Very interesting," John replied. "We people in the West also have stories. Some say that our forefathers were *pagi* (little furry animals), and that gives us the right to act like *pagi*. In reality, God created everything. God made us like himself, so that we might have fellowship with him. Our forefathers knew this truth, but they wanted to do their own thing. They were deceived by evil spirits and no longer taught their children about God. After many generations the knowledge of God was lost.

"Even so, God still loved his people, the ones he had created. He came into this world. He became like one of us. When he grew up, he taught us; he showed us what God was like. Then he proved his love for us by taking the punishment for our wrongdoing upon himself. He died for us, but he came back to life. He said that he was returning to Heaven, but that he would come to earth again. In the meantime we are to tell everyone about his love and his ways."

Then John added something that boggled their minds. "You and I are related. We have the same forefathers, the same ones who were deceived by the evil spirits and lost their knowledge of God." They stopped and looked at each other and then at John in astonishment.

"You and we—we are related? We have a common ancestry?"

This news spread quickly from hamlet to hamlet.

Wuninip and two other Danis began to meet with John every morning. Soon others joined them. "We, too, want to hear *kiwone*."

During these first few months John and Helen had no way of knowing what was going on in the hearts of the influential Dani leaders who were listening to *kiwone*. Several of these men, who lived far away, built huts in Kanggime and stayed during the week. On weekends they walked back to their villages. With little to do during the week, they often crowded into the Dekkers' house, wanting to talk with John. If he wasn't there, they would wait, making things difficult for Helen.

"Would you please move a bit. I'm trying to prepare Ndeka's meal," she pleaded as she struggled to clear a space to work at the wood stove. When John arrived he said, "Come on, men, let's go over to my office." There they questioned him endlessly.

Soon John suggested to them a plan that had been pioneered effectively in the Ilaga Valley by Don Gibbons,[1] John Ellenberger, and Gordon Larson, missionaries of the Christian and Missionary Alliance, and by Dave Martin at Karubaga.

"You go home to your villages and appoint representatives to come for teaching four days each week in a witness school. You choose leaders who show a desire to listen to God's words and to follow them. Each Friday these *aap tekola* (students) will return to their villages and teach others the Bible lessons and Scripture verses they learn. In this way several hundred will learn rather than a few.

"*Wa! Wa!*" (expression of appreciation), they responded excitedly.

First they had to help build a teaching house, a round building fifteen feet in diameter. There they chose their village representatives to the witness school.

John had little teaching material in the Dani language. Some basic Bible verses had been translated by Gordon Larson in the Ilaga and had been mimeographed. A Dani alphabet and a Dani primer were in process. Bill Mallon of Karubaga had some of the language written down, and John had scribblers full of his own language notes. Two years before, Don Richter of Gospel Recordings had come through the Ilaga district and made recordings in Dani. John had purchased several records, and in these early days of learning the difficult Dani language they were of great help.

He spent long hours in lesson preparation, trying to find

the right words for each of the truths he wanted to teach. He could not find a word for *love* but discovered one which meant "my heart is joined to yours," and that worked well. He found that the Dani language is not a primitive collection of grunts as some might expect of Stone-Age people. Rather, it is a highly structured, complex system, frequently with more accurate shades of meaning than English.

Early on Tuesday, as soon as the mist cleared from the mountains, fifteen *aap tekola* left their villages and gathered in the teaching house. John sat on a small stump; his students squatted on leaves or pieces of wood on the ground. John looked at the men in his class. He recognized most of them and knew many by name. *There's Wuninip.* John had expected him. *And Muta's uncle, Tekola!* He was in his forties and the oldest in the class. John saw Noonit and Wimili and many other men he had worked with. They ranged in age from teens to Tekola. All were greased and their long hair held in nets. They wore the usual ornamental arm bands and the gourd. That was all. But in their faces he saw curiosity and expectancy—or was it hunger for something to satisfy their unsatisfying existence? *They will not be disappointed! Lord, help me to find the right words to make plain your truth.*

On that first day of class John started with the account of creation. Using Gordon Larson's notes, the students memorized together, "In the beginning God created the heavens and the earth" (Genesis 1:1). John added things in their culture that they could relate to: pigs, potatoes, dogs, and the moon and the stars. He used a simple storytelling method. He repeated, because the Dani had no background in theology, and his language ability was limited.

"In the beginning God created the heavens and the earth. *Wakkagagerak* (Creator) is his name. Say it again. And again. You say it, Wuninip. Now you, Bitbet. Tonight when you are eating your *mbingga* (sweet potato greens) teach it to your wives and children. When you sit around in the men's house, teach it to your friends."

After class they went off to work, usually in a group, cutting wood or building fences, improving their trails or working on their gardens.

On the second day John opened with review. "Let's say our verse again. 'In the beginning God created the heavens and the earth.'" They all joined in.

"What do you think it means?"

"He made all we can see—for instance, the *laluragan*," a Dani suggested.

"What do you mean by that?" John probed.

"Those little lights up in the sky."

"Do you know what they are?"

"They are fireflies, or the place fireflies come from."

Then John gave them a lesson on the stars. "God made them all," he emphasized.

"Now I am going to teach you a new verse. 'God created man in his own image. Male and female created he them'" (Genesis 1:27). They memorized it and talked about it.

Then John asked them a question. "Is there a difference between man and animals?"

"Sure," they answered quickly.

"What?"

"We can talk, and we are smarter than animals."

Another added, "We always kill them and eat them, but they seldom kill us."

Another backed up the claim by describing the wild pig. "It is very dangerous. It can hurt us, but almost never kills us."

At the next class session John told them about the fall of man. "Our ancestors' names were Adam and Eve. They listened to Satan, the chief of the evil spirits."

One of the students spoke up. "We, too, have a very bad spirit who has existed as long as anyone can remember. His name is Monggat, and he sits on the foreheads of men and leads them to do all kinds of evil. Monggat's wife lives in the hearts of the women and causes them to do wrong things too. They also have children who live on the foreheads of our children, and in plains and forests."

John was glad for this bit of information concerning Dani beliefs. He continued, "Satan was created as a beautiful angel, but he chose to rebel against God and to do things his way. Some of the other beautiful angels followed him in this evil. One day Satan came to our ancestors in the form of a snake and persuaded them also to follow his bad ways. Adam and Eve could have lived forever, because they had eternal life; but they listened to the chief evil spirit and did what he told them to do. As a result they lost the secret of eternal life.

"'When Adam sinned, sin entered the entire human race. His sin spread death throughout all the world, so everything began to grow old and to die, for all have sinned'" (Romans 5:12, TLB). They memorized the verse.

"*Wa! wa!* That is a good story. Our ancestors, too, could have lived forever," the Danis responded, but somehow the secret of eternal life was lost to them. "The snake has the secret. He can shed his old skin and get a new one, and he never seems to die.

"Long ago, our ancestors saw a snake coming from the direction of where our ancestors had come from—where the sun comes up. As the snake slithered along, he was whispering '*nabelan-kabelan, nabelan-kabelan*' (my skin, your skin; my skin, your skin).

"Our forefathers were excited: the snake is saying, 'As my skin is, so yours can become. You too can have the secret of eternal life!' Then a little black and white bird swooped in from the same direction. '*Piriwak nalop kalop! Pirik! Pirik! Pirik!* (mud on you, mud on you),' the bird mocked. Our forefathers decided he was talking about our custom of covering ourselves with mud as a sign of mourning. 'Is the bird saying that death will remain with us?' they wondered. 'Yet the snake is ready to tell us the secret of living forever. What can all this mean?'

"Both creatures moved in the same direction, but the

bird quickly outdistanced the snake. As our ancestors argued, the bird flew away. Then they saw that the snake, too, was gone. They were left with death."

Another Dani spoke. "If the *pirogobit* bird had not shown scorn, the snake would have shared the secret of eternal life. But now he refuses to. This is why we despise the *pirogobit* bird. But the snake comes from our ancestors with the secret of eternal life, so we will not kill it," the Danis explained. John saw an opportunity to relate God's truth to their story and to them.

"That is a most interesting *mbynypak*," John agreed, "but it was not a little bird who deceived your ancestors and robbed them of the truth. It was really demons, evil spirits. Satan, the chief evil spirit, is a liar and a thief and a murderer. He has put murder into the hearts of people. He makes you fight among yourselves because he wants to destroy you.

"But listen. God spoke to Satan and told him, 'I'm going to crush your head. I'm going to give my people eternal life once more.'"

At the next class they reviewed and reviewed. Early in each session, while minds were fresh, they memorized a new key verse.

"'All have sinned and come short of the glory of God' (Romans 3:23, KJV). Now you tell me what that means. How does it relate to your life?" John asked.

"Yes, we know we are sinners. We have killed people, burned their houses, killed their pigs."

"But what does it mean to 'come short of the glory of God?'" John asked. They didn't respond. He continued, "We come short when we don't measure up to the character of God, when we don't act toward others the way God would act, or pity others the way God pities them.

"When you lie about a person, you rob that person of his dignity and his worth. You can even murder a man or a woman with your tongue when you lie about him. Some of you have said because you saw a woman close to where a man was that she must have put a spell on him. You say, 'I saw her give him a potato, and now he is sick—she must have put poison on it.' Then the people kill that woman, because you told a lie.

"We are not to steal from each other. We are not to kill each other. We are to respect each other, because we all are made in the image of God. God loves people, and we should love them too.

"Do you understand this?" John asked.

"Yes, yes."

"You must pass on what I have taught you. Tell your friends this weekend. You must give it away. You have God's words; now you must give them to others. If you are not willing to share this good news with others, don't bother to come back next week!" John challenged. Out they went two by two to all the surrounding hamlets to share what they had learned.

On Tuesday morning the *aap tekola* returned. "How was it?" John asked.

"*Abu obeelom kogorak!* (We found it really good!)," the Danis replied. "The people listened to us. They want *kiwone.*"

"Let's go on." Dekker assembled his student-teachers. "God, the Creator, came and lived among men to show us what he is like. His name when he walked among us was Jesus, the Creator. He showed us by his character that he is holy and good and kind. Remember last week I taught you that all of us are made in the image of God. God made *you* to be like him. You are important to God. He wants *you* to be his child and to be just like him. Our forefather, Adam, was kind and good at first, but he lost most of this because he sinned in the garden. Traces of the Creator's likeness are still in you even though your people have long forgotten about God. You have strayed. God hasn't heard from you for a long time. You have sinned. All people in the world have sinned—turned away from God.

"God did not turn his back on us. We turned our backs on him. We wanted to do things our way. Our wrongs separated us from God.

"But he still loves us. He loves you. God proved his love when he took on himself all our wrongs, so that once more we can come close to God and know what he is like. Because we are made in God's image, we need to be like him to be truly happy.

"Let's memorize these verses: 'Christ [the Creator] died for our sins . . . he was buried and he rose again' (1 Corinthians 15, 3, 4, KJV). 'For as in Adam all die, so in Christ [the Creator] all will be made alive' (1 Corinthians 15:22, NIV)."

There was more teaching, more memorizing of Scripture verses. After another four days of two-hour lessons, the Danis again went out over the mountains, repeating what they had learned. Occasionally the message got garbled, sometimes due to their not understanding, sometimes because John was a novice in the language.

Recognizing the possibility of misunderstanding, he went out to the villages from time to time on the weekends. In the evenings he walked among the huts and listened to the men repeat what they had learned.

"I'm outside listening to what you're saying!" he told them.

"Come in," they urged, and that gave him opportunity to correct mistakes.

No furnishings enhanced the circular huts. There was no lamp, not even a candle, only a fire in the center. The men sat cross-legged on a reed floor or on pieces of wood on the dirt floor and leaned against the wall. Perhaps they roasted a few potatoes or cobs of corn as they talked. They had their main meal of *mbingga* at the women's houses at four or five o'clock. Then, after sundown, they congregated in the men's houses, where they whiled away the evening swapping stories. Now their talk was taken up with the new *kiwone*.

"Tell us again how we are made in God's image, and how we have the same ancestor as you," they requested as John joined their firesides.

"That is true. You and I were made by the Creator, in

his image. We have the same ancestors. Many moons have passed since that time, and we have become different. We know things you don't, and you know things we don't. You have many advantages over us. You can walk on the trails by the light of the stars, but we need to carry a light. You can walk barefoot, but we need shoes. Your women carry heavy loads; ours cannot.

"God still has a claim on you, because he made you. You still are a people made in his image, although that image is largely lost because your forefathers were so deceived that they stopped talking about God. Those who came after them were further deceived, and didn't even know that there is a God or a Satan. Now you people think only about yourselves.

"Although you have forgotten God, he hasn't forgotten you. He still loves you. He prepared me to come and tell you about God the Creator. God spoke to me and said, 'Others are made in my image; you must go and tell them about me.'"

"What about *nabelan-kabelan*?" they asked. "How can we get a 'new skin' and live forever? We do not want to die."

The threat of death was terrible in the Dani world. Surrounded by wailing relatives, the dying person lay on a mat on a cold dirt floor with no covering, no relief from pain, and no nourishment if unable to eat.

"My friends, because Adam, our forefather, sinned, his body grew old and died. Our bodies eventually will grow old and will die, but God has given us a spirit that will live forever. Someday God will give us new bodies like Christ's body. We will live forever!

"Satan wants to destroy our lives. The Creator wants to give us new life. God's children listen to God's talk. Satan's children listen to Satan's talk. Will you listen to God's talk, or go on listening to Satan's talk?"

One night the men said to him, "You have learned our talk quickly. You eat our potatoes. You sleep in our huts. You are now one of us here. You call yourself Ndeka, but that means nothing to us so we want to give you a name we understand. We want to name you after the Toli River. Your name shall be *Tolibaga!* And your wife shall be called *Tukwe* (path woman)."

One day a Dani came to John. "I really want to follow after Jesus. Will you please write down my name?"

"Why do you want me to write down your name?" John asked.

"I want to go on record that I will follow after Jesus Christ."

"OK, if that's what you want, I'll take down your name," John agreed. The next day several others came by with the same request. "Why do you want me to do this?" John asked, still trying to find out what was prompting this action. "Never mind, just write down our names. We want to give you these sweet potatoes as our thanks."

Every day in the late afternoon some Danis came by to ask John to record their names. After some time he realized that these Danis equated his writing their names with having their names written in the Book of Life.

"I don't think we should continue this," John explained. "My writing your names won't help you. Your names must be written in Heaven by the angels or the Lord himself."

Another incident occurred during those early days. Yiganggan, one of the witness men, had a vision of his deceased father who told him the people should make new houses because the old round huts were so dirty from soot and pigs. Yiganggan mentioned this to his people, who decided that they would build new houses, but they would be low, rectangular structures like the ones which the Danis who worked for the missionaries had built. These had a cooking area at the front and sleeping quarters at the rear. While it was true that with no fire in the center, the house was not blackened with smoke, neither was it as warm. The Danis had no blankets and almost perished from cold. They had not considered that the Dekkers gave blankets to their Dani workers living in rectangular houses.

This idea of building rectangular houses was picked up, added to, and twisted into error. In one village a Dani man secretly bought an ax head, then showed it to the people, telling them that the spirits had brought it to him during the night. "Our forefathers are coming back, and they will bring us many goods—salt, knives, axes, and towels. We must build new, clean longhouses to receive them."

When this indigenous cargo cult spread to several villages, Wuninip and other Christian Dani leaders took a strong stand against it. One of the new houses burned down, then another, and before long the whole thing was forgotten.

7 "O Creator, Greetings"

Tolibaga continued teaching, building on what he had taught before. "God the Creator showed his character in many ways when he walked among men on earth. One way was by telling stories." And John told these stories in terms familiar to the Danis. He told about a warrior who had been hit by an arrow and left for dead while the war moved on past him.

"Another warrior came along, not one of his own clan, and heard the injured warrior groaning. This warrior could have hurried on his way to get out of the dangerous war zone. It wasn't his problem to look after the man who had been hurt, but he stopped and dragged the hurting man into the bushes and out of sight. He checked the man's wounds, then put him on his shoulders and carried him to a warm hut where there was a fire and someone who would look after him.[1]

"The Creator taught that we should help other people, not just those of our own clan. We are to care for one another. We are to be a blessing to others. Because we are made in his image, we are to do as he would do."

Day after day John taught the witness men and a few women who had joined the class. None of the Danis could read or write, yet they could memorize a whole paragraph word for

word as he taught it to them. Most of the lessons were from the
life of Christ, but at the same time he taught historical seg-
ments on Adam and Eve and Abraham, explaining that the
first eleven chapters of Genesis are an introduction to the
whole Bible.

"Take Abraham. We can't fully know what God wants
from us if we don't understand the story of Abraham and see
how God walks with men. Abraham lived thousands of years
ago, but even so we can relate to him because the Bible calls
Abraham the father of all who believe. 'Those who have faith
are blessed along with Abraham' (Galatians 3:7, 9, NIV).
Abraham lived among people who did not worship the true
God. They worshiped other gods and spirits and offered sacrifices." With this his listeners identified.

"God had given Abraham many pigs and gardens. He
was an influential man, a leader in his clan. But because some
of his people worshiped evil spirits, God could not bless
Abraham the way he wanted to. God told Abraham: 'Go out of
the place where you live and feel comfortable, the place where
you have grown up and know everybody. Go away from the
people who do not honor me to a place where I can talk to you,
and I will bless you.' Abraham turned his back on the old ways
and obeyed God.

"You Danis have grown up with fighting, and have
feared the spirits. You have had your fetishes. Now you have
put aside that way of life. God has called you out of your bondage to the spirits and all that kept you from fellowship with
him. Now God says to you, 'I want to talk to you. I want to
bless you with my presence.' *At nen kinom aret ogotip o'* (He
himself is with you). He wants you to live a life of joy. He
wants to bless you so you can be a blessing to the people around
you. Unless you share the good things God has given to you,
they'll do you little good."

The following day John continued with the story of
Abraham.

"Sometimes too many people live in one place, and

there isn't room for them all." The Danis nodded. When there was not enough land for their gardens, fighting would start, and some were forced to relocate. It had happened to their fathers.

"In the case of Abraham, God had blessed him and his relatives with so many pigs and gardens there wasn't enough room for everyone. Rather than getting in a fight, Abraham said to his nephew Lot, 'You choose where you want to live.' He gave Lot the first choice.

"Lot should have said to his older uncle, 'God will look after me; *you* choose first.' Instead, he grabbed the best place in the valley for himself. When bad people living in that valley started to fight Lot, Abraham could have said, 'That's your problem, you chose to go there.' Instead Abraham helped Lot. He fought Lot's enemies until they ran away. And though Abraham's gardens were on rocky ground, God continued to bless him with big potatoes, because Abraham followed God. His character was in line with God's character.

"Sometimes Abraham made mistakes. He was a man like you and me," John told them in the next lesson. "One day he gave his wife to another man and said she was his sister, just to save his own skin. Now this was not what God wanted Abraham to do, but God was patient with him. He did not turn his back on him. God still walked with him and talked with him. Sometimes we make mistakes and we think God will turn his back on us. He still wants to be with us on the trails and in our houses. We can share our burdens with him because he is a true friend. We can follow him; he knows the way.

"God gave Abraham many good things, but not a child." The Danis looked sorrowful. "Abraham waited for this blessing for many years. He didn't give up. He kept working in the gardens, and cutting down trees. Finally God gave him a son. Abraham was very proud as the baby grew into a strong young boy. One day God said to Abraham, 'You must take this son and sacrifice him.'"

The Danis gasped. "How is this possible? How could God ask a man to do this?"

"You haven't heard the end of the story," John told them. "God tests us, but not more than we can bear. He may never test another man in this way. This was the hardest thing that had ever happened in Abraham's life. He had decided to follow the Lord. He had left his own people. He had made mistakes. But God had blessed him because he was following God. Was he going to say *no* to God now?"

The Danis weren't sure they wanted him to say *yes*. They loved their children.

"Abraham strongly believed that God could bring his son back to life again—that's how strong our God is. Abraham made a special place of sacrifice, an altar, and laid his son on it. Then he took his knife and was ready to plunge it into his son when God spoke: 'Stop, Abraham! Now I know you love me and will obey and trust me. Take your boy off the altar. Here is a little animal; kill it instead.'"

The Danis had become very tense. They sighed in relief.

"God's purposes are always good, and not evil," John assured them. "If we are to learn about God, however, we need to be tested. We need to stretch our faith. God brings difficulties into our lives, even sickness and death. In these we can experience God's strengthening and grace. God said to Abraham: 'Because you obeyed me, because you trusted me, and were willing to give me your only son, I'm going to bless you with as many children as there are stars in the sky!'"

The Dani men turned their heads from side to side in amazement and noisily clicked their gourds with long fingernails. "*Ayee! Ayee!* So many sons!"

From the beginning John stressed stewardship—of the truth God has given, of time, strength, and material possessions. He believed that this teaching needed to be basic to the Danis' concept of the Christian life—that he should not wait until they were more mature Christians. He emphasized that God's truth and his blessings must be shared with others. It followed naturally his teaching on the work of Christ on the cross. "You were bought at a price. Therefore honor God with your body" (1 Corinthians 6:20, NIV). "Therefore, I urge you, brothers, in view of God's mercy, to offer your bodies as living sacrifices, holy and pleasing to God" (Romans 12:1, NIV).

After covering the subject of stewardship in several sessions, he asked questions to see what they were getting out of the teaching.

"What does God want most for you to offer to him?"

"*Nineebe* (our bodies)," Wuninip answered.

"Very good! If you offer yourself, what are some things you can do that will show you have done this?"

"We'll do what Christ wants us to do," said Tekola.

"Give me an example."

"We will help people to know the Good News."

"What about sharing with those who used to be your enemies?" They had to think about that.

"They need it too. We are already sharing the truth with them."

"What is the truth that you must share?"

"That we must not kill each other. That God loves us all."

"What are some of the blessings you must share?"

"*Kiwone*," answered one. "We must help our enemies across the river to build a good bridge so they won't fall in the river," added another.

The Danis accepted the teaching on stewardship and began to apply it.

John never pressed for decisions in classes or meetings. If he had asked, "Who would like to accept Christ?" all would put up their hands. He had learned that the Danis do everything by consensus. It had been a group decision to burn their fetishes and stop their wars and a group decision to listen to God's teaching. When he was alone with a Dani, he challenged him to make a personal decision for full commitment.

Unbelievers showed no active resistance to John. At first the witness men were not received in some areas, but that didn't last long.

One day John decided it was time to try to teach them the song, "Come into My Heart, Lord Jesus." He first explained, "The eternal life we all want is not just physical life. It is not only our spirit that lives forever; it is God living in us, giving us *his* life." They liked the chorus, but they had a difficult time singing the melody. Instead of trying to teach Western songs, he decided to start them composing songs in the five-note Dani style in which they sing and chant a little story. He led off:

"You are God." The Danis chorused, "Jesu, Jesu!"
"You have come."
"Jesu, Jesu!"
"You love us so."
"Jesu, Jesu!"
"You died for us."
"Jesu, Jesu!"

The Danis could go on for dozens of verses. They liked John to lead the singing. They liked him to do anything their way—eating their potatoes, sleeping in their huts, singing their songs. But soon he put a Dani in the song-leading role. Before long they were singing Bible truths and verses as they worked in the gardens or walked the trails.

"I can see changes in the Danis. It is like a flower opening," Helen observed one day. "I see it in their eyes, in the way they walk and talk. They are beginning to show consideration for others, a patience that was not present before. They are becoming more loving and gentle, less self-centered. And they aren't always pestering me!"

Wuninip continued to come to John's office, asking questions. He also attended the witness classes faithfully. When Wuninip spoke, people were quiet and listened. When

Tolibaga asked a question and Wuninip answered, it was always well thought-out, spoken rapidly and persuasively. Every weekend he and the witness men went to other clans to share what they had learned during the week.

Several months passed before Wuninip knew he was a new creature in Christ. John realized it when he heard Wuninip pray, "*Wakkagagerak Kawonak!* (O Creator, greetings!). I come to you in appreciation that you have made me in your image. I thank you that you brought Tolibaga to us. I thank you for forgiving my sins."

Wuninip could have said, "Thank you that we are never going to die," thinking they had found the physical *nabelan-kabelan*. Or he could have been happy simply for all the axes and knives he was getting. It was obvious that the Word of God was in Wuninip's heart.

In the Dani language the word for *believe* carries the meaning of hearing and doing—of *obeying*. A believer is one who has heard, received, and acted on God's Word. If there is no change in a professed believer's life, he is only a hearer. John was certain that Wuninip was a believer. He and other Dani believers became witnesses to what God had done in their lives. Like the blind man Jesus healed, they said, "This one thing we know—once we were blind, but now we see. God has changed us!"

The Danis in John and Helen's house staff also were changed. In addition to teaching the witness school, John held class for his own "household"—for Leleki, Muta, the faithful young Dani man who took care of the grounds, and the youngsters who regularly carried wood, swept floors, or peeled potatoes. For half an hour after lunch each day they sat in John's office while he gave them the same Bible lessons he taught in the witness school.

"I feel a little like Abraham," he confided to Helen, "but I want to help those who help us in the house, and to be a blessing to them as they are to us."

8 Breakthroughs

John approached the literacy program with his usual vigor and sense of urgency. *We may not have much time to establish the Dani church. We may not have next week!* The political situation in the country was far from secure. With Indonesia and the Netherlands scrapping over rights to the west end of the island, all Dutch citizens had been repatriated. Though John had become a Canadian citizen, he was afraid that all Westerners might be forced to leave. Before that happened—if it did—he wanted to teach the Danis to read and to write.

In the witness class, John had emphasized that the Bible is not his word. "It is God's Word." Because in the past, under witchcraft, only the shaman had access to the magic incantations, to read *kiwone* themselves was what Dani believers wanted most. From the start many Danis wanted to learn to read and to write—especially those in the witness class. John was anxious to begin lessons as soon as the Dani primers were ready.

A literacy committee had been at work for a year, preparing literacy materials. Now the results of their work were available. When the Dani language primers arrived in Kanggime, the fifteen men in the witness class became the first literacy class. Even Tekola, age forty-eight, took the challenge. Primer One introduced some letters of the alphabet and some simple words such as *mo* (sun), *me* (place), and *en* (sugar cane). Quickly the students went through the first primer and moved on to the second, where they learned how to put two words together.

"*An na* (I go)," they said over and over.

By this time others were wanting to learn. "You teach them," John told the first class. They put up a larger rectangular building with ten rooms for the ten levels of literacy. The Primer Three group taught the Primer One group while forging ahead to Primer Four. The Primer Six students passed on what they had learned to the Primer Four group. Each grade learned and taught.

As in any class in any country, some were slower learners than others; but most caught on quickly and showed a high intelligence. Within six months they had gone through all ten levels and were reading well. Graduates went out to start literacy schools in other village centers.

More clamored to enroll. Students ranged in age from children to forty years, but the majority were teens and young married adults. About 120 were involved in the program at one time, resulting in increased demand for notebooks and pencils. John looked around for another make-work project— one that even the children could do to pay for precious school materials. He didn't need to look far. For years the Danis had been cutting down trees, first to clear the land for their huge gardens, then for firewood and for building fences and houses. The mountainside behind the Dekker house was practically denuded.

"Muta, the children can work on reforestation. You make that your project. Have the children find little trees in the forest and teach them how to plant the trees on the hillside." Then John instructed the village elders, "No one is to cut this new forest. Your children will be living here after you.

They will need these trees for firewood and to build houses and fences. By planting now, their needs will be met."

After the emergency appendectomy in March, and the blood poisoning which followed, Helen had looked forward to a time of renewed strength—*by summer surely,* she thought. But summer had come and the new strength had not. Instead her weight had dropped from 110 to eighty-eight pounds, and she felt worse. During these months Paul and Eva had picked up impetigo from the Dani children, and the miserable rash required constant attention to give them relief. Along with that, Eva contracted a severe ear infection which nearly developed into encephalitis. In panic they had flown her to the coast.

As this was the time the literacy program was getting underway, John was immersed in classes and projects, as well as traveling to the villages. Helen was often alone except for the babies. Anxiety over the children and her own worsening physical condition accentuated the loneliness.

"I can't stand not having anyone to talk to. You have your friend, Wuninip, but I have no one," she complained to John.

John could see that what she said was true, though he could not completely relate to her problem. He had never experienced loneliness. More than that, he didn't know what to do about it.

"Helen, if I spent more time at home, who would do the work with the Danis—the Bible teaching, the literacy classes, the counseling, visiting the villages, and the development projects? With the political situation the way it is, I'm afraid that any day we will hear that we must leave. We need to establish a church before that happens."

Helen understood this, but that didn't help her physical condition or the interminable days without conversation. She determined to take the initiative—she would go with John on his next trek over the hills. Because her feet were not conditioned to long walks, the result was painful blisters, making it almost impossible for her to go on. When sunstroke caused nausea, there was no way she could continue. The Danis made a stretcher of laced vines hung between two poles and carried her on it. It worked until they were on the steeper slopes with sharp turns. Then she slid off as the Danis had to maneuver the stretcher in near-vertical positions to follow the trail's terrain. Lack of success in this venture added to her growing sense of failure.

By September she was weaker and having fainting spells. The mission doctor diagnosed her problem as psychosomatic. "Helen is rejecting life with the Danis. Subconsciously she wants to return to America."

"But that is not so!" It was true that she felt guilty because some things about the Danis irritated her and bothered her out of all proportion. Neither was she doing well learning the language. Burdened with failure and guilt, besides physical weakness, she at times would have given anything to get out of her situation. Yet, she knew beyond doubt that God had arranged her marriage to John, and his heart was with the Danis. They had adopted him as one of their own, had even named him Tolibaga. No, she would not accept that she was rejecting the call. "I do not want to forsake the work God has called us to."

The contradictory thoughts and feelings gnawed away, and one day they spilled out. "John, I can't stand another minute of this. I can't stand the dirt and the people always pushing around me. The climate is so terrible—it's cold and dark—and it rains all the time!"

"But, Helen, the sun shines every day!"

As each reflected on the other's statement, they realized both were true. It did rain virtually every day, but the sun shone each day too.

"I see the rain and you see only the sun. That's the way it always it—everything is wonderful for you. You are always happy with the Danis and your work, and I am so miserable!"

They went to the coast for further tests, only to hear the doctors agree with the earlier diagnosis. Helen and John were devastated.

"John, what's wrong with me? Am I losing my mind? Oh, John, I don't want to leave the work. You do believe me, don't you?"

John did not feel that her problems were "all psychological." But he was confused about the whole situation. It was clear to him that they could not stay with Helen's health as it was; yet he knew God had sent them there. For the first time, John questioned, "What's going on, Lord? We've been at Kanggime only nine months. People are responding to your Word. Is this an attack from the enemy who is losing ground where he has had unchallenged control? Surely you didn't send us all this distance only for us to leave after so short a time. Please show me the answer!"

In the hot little house where rats and cockroaches added to their despair, they searched their hearts, their relationship to God, and to each other. John felt that he hadn't helped Helen in her aloneness, but neither did he see how he could have and worked with the Danis too.

The heavens seemed closed to their pleas for direction.

"Oh, John, you're always so well, and I'm falling apart. I've failed you so badly!" Tears took over.

To pack and go home seemed the only alternative. The mission had assigned a couple to look after the work at Kanggime. Sadly John and Helen wrote to their supporters that they must leave Daniland. The speedy responses bore the same message: "Don't leave. God is going to raise up Helen."

Knowing that these people were standing with them in their trial penetrated Helen's feeling of defeat and John's disappointment. Then came the first tangible sign that God was working. A visitor appeared at the little house where they teetered between decisions to go or to stay in New Guinea.

It was Armia Heikenen, headmistress of the Christian and Missionary Alliance school. "Helen, I heard about your problem and feel that I may be able to help. You may be experiencing what I did after I had been in New Guinea a while. Has your metabolism been checked?"

"No, I was to have the test, but the hospital's equipment is broken."

"Helen, you may have an iodine deficiency. You probably have noticed that many of the Dani women have goiters resulting from the lack of iodine in the soil of some areas. These women eat mainly sweet potatoes grown in that soil. Have you also—"

"Yes, we eat a lot of sweet potatoes!"

Armia handed her some kelp tablets. "Try these."

In only two days Helen noticed a change.

"John, I feel better!"

When she continued to improve, they radioed Jacques and Ruth Teeuwen who were filling in for them at Kanggime. "We're coming back!"

"Tolibaga and Tukwe are coming!" The Teeuwens had shared the news with the Dani believers who gathered at the airstrip to welcome their river man and path woman. As the *wururu* (airplane) circled the airstrip for the landing, Tolibaga and Tukwe looked down on the crowd waiting for them. The Danis were jumping up and down with excitement! John prayed, "Dear Lord, these are your people made in your image. Thank you for sending us back into Kanggime, this place of evil spirits and death, this stronghold of Satan. It's time for that bondage to end. Soon the chains will snap and these prisoners will go free. They'll walk as kings and priests before you, witnesses to the whole world of your mighty power and love. O God, overrule our weakness. Give us the wisdom we desperately lack. Bring understanding to the Dani hearts. We know that we can make an impact on the people only through the Spirit of God. You have said, 'Not by might, nor by power, but by my Spirit'" (Zechariah 4:6).

The Danis first celebration of God the Creator coming into the world was a day of great festivity. Some walked two hours from over the mountains, carrying string net bags bulging with food for the feast. Each hamlet had killed a pig and gutted it. The animal was slung over the headman's shoulder or, if too big, carried on a pole between two men. Singing and chanting, the Danis came over the trails, until nearly a thousand arrived for the first Christmas feast.

Days earlier the men had dug cooking pits, one for each clan or hamlet, and had gathered firewood and rocks. Early on feast day the rocks were placed on the wood. Fire was taken from the coals in a nearby hut and blown into a flame to light the wood. Then with forked sticks the heated rocks were maneuvered into the cooking pits, which had been lined with leaves and grasses. Sweet potatoes with their leaves and vines, cobs of corn, and cut-up pigs were placed on top of the hot stones. More stones were rolled in, and another layer of *mbingga* (sweet potato greens) was added. Water was sprinkled over all, and finally the larger leaves were folded in and weighted down with rocks. By noon all the pits were sealed and the food began to cook.

Meanwhile, John told the Christmas story. "God so loved the world that he gave his only Son. The Creator God became a baby, like little Nop." John patted the head of the Dani child who had toddled over and was clinging to his leg. "God came to us because he loves us and to show us what he is like. He wants us to be like him, which is how he made us in the first place. The Creator God grew to be a little boy, playing like your children do. Then he became a man and went into the forest to cut down trees. He made houses with the wood. Then one day, to prove how much he loved us, he died and took on himself the punishment for all our sins—all the wrongs we have done or ever will do and he died on a cross. He did this so we could have his life in us and be restored to the image of our heavenly Father. But he didn't stay in the grave—he came to life again. Once more he walked over the trails and talked with his friends. He made a fire and cooked a feast for them. He promised that one day he will come back to earth. Then he went back to Heaven."

When John had finished speaking, Wuninip stood up. "That is good talk Tolibaga brings to us. Many of us have never sat down together, because we fought each other for so long." Then Wuninip prayed.

"*Wakkagagerak, kawonak!* (O Creator, greetings). We never knew you existed, but here we are. Greetings! We always used to fight and kill each other, but you brought us together. Greetings! Thank you for your Word. Thank you for sending Tolibaga. We have burned our fetishes. We have stopped our wars. Now we will listen to you, O *Wakkagagerak*, greetings!"

Then they ate. Around three o'clock little groups began leaving for their homes, carrying the leftover food with them, and singing as they went, "*Wagagendak, wa!* (Thank you, Jesus, thank you for coming!)."

RBMU was planning another pioneer outreach, this one to the cannibalistic Yali people.[1] Stanley Dale and Bruno de Leeuw had gone there to build the airstrip necessary to establish a base. Several Dani believers from the Toli area had accompanied them six months earlier, not only to work on the strip, but also to make friends with the local tribespeople. Nggati was outstanding in this ministry of "helps."

"You people should listen to the Word of God instead of depending on the evil spirits," he challenged Yalis in an effort to prepare the way for the missionaries.

Because building the airstrip there had been a long and difficult project, John offered to help. Since the capable Teeuwens had remained at Kanggime to study the language, he felt he could leave Kanggime for a short period.

John had been gone a week when Helen was awakened at midnight by Eva's cries. *I'll warm a bottle for her*, Helen decided. As she stepped into the hall, she was startled to see flames consuming the whole kitchen wall. There had been nothing to make her suspect fire—no smell of smoke, no heat. Even now there was only a faint crackling sound. Helen quickly called to waken Muta, who without a word rushed to the children's room, jumped out of the window, and reached up to receive little Paul and baby Eva as Helen handed them to him. Helen then jumped to the ground herself. As she turned to run around the house to enter the front door, Muta called, "Don't go that way!" She had forgotten the cans of metholated spirits in the attic. She turned back to see flames enveloping the entire house.

Jacques Teeuwen rushed toward the house. "No, Jacques, no! We are safe!" As the Teeuwens and sympathetic Danis gathered around, Helen cried. Irreplaceable treasures— wedding and baby photos, gifts made by loving hands—were consumed, but her tears expressed relief. *You have spared me and my babies. Thank you, thank you, Jesus.*

Please God, control this fire! Don't let it spread to other homes, Ruth Teeuwen prayed while the flames reached up and out. Another danger got their attention. Flames were approaching the bark walls of the washhouse twelve feet from the burning house.

"Stay away!" Helen called out to the Danis who were milling nearby. She knew that against the washhouse wall were two large drums, one containing kerosene and the other aviation fuel. "Stay away from the drums," she screamed.

Suddenly, to the missionaries' horror, they saw some Danis actually standing on the fuel drums as they tried to beat out the flames of the burning washhouse.

"Come away! Come away!" Helen cried, but they could not hear her above the roar of the fire and their own excited yells to one another.

"We must get Tolibaga's tools! And the radio!" The Danis tore off strips of bark from the wall to enter the flaming washhouse. They shoved Helen's washing machine away from the blaze and locked John's tools in the chicken yard so no one could steal them. Triumphantly they carried the radio to Helen, who was very grateful.

The Danis had not realized, however, that the radio would not work without its battery. Jacques slipped into the building through the hole in the wall. "I'm afraid it's unusable." He returned with the blackened battery. "But they saved your washing machine, Helen, and John's tools."

Through it all, the Danis showed incredible bravery. Earlier they had even tried to enter the blazing main house. Because of their efforts, most of the washhouse was saved. Helen and the Teeuwens stood looking at the drums, blackened and bulging from internal pressure, but still intact. Prayers of thanksgiving went heavenward.

"You have lost so much—why aren't you crying?" the Danis asked as they crowded around Helen. "The Dekkers have a big house in Jesus' yard. The things that really count cannot be destroyed," Jacques Teeuwen explained.

First thing in the morning they tried the radio. In Ninia John tuned in the portable unit at the scheduled contact time. "Our house has burned. The children are all right. Please come home." He was barely able to hear Helen's message.

The transmission was faint; the impact of the brief message was not. "Thank you, Lord, for saving Helen and the children," was his first response. Dealing with the bad news was more difficult. *The house—gone!* The news penetrated deep, evoking a mixture of questions and agitation. *No time for this now.* After arranging for a plane to meet him, he gathered up his few belongings and with two Danis began the treacherous two-day trip to the nearest landing strip. *I wonder what they were able to save. Part of the house? Some of the things in it? Why speculate?* The turbulence of mind gave way to peace, knowing that all was in God's hands. Spurred on by the desire to get home, he outdid his usual fast trek and made the trip in one day, surprising even the Danis who knew he was good on the trail. From the airstrip he was flown to Kanggime.

It was a depressing sight. Nothing remained of the house. "How did the fire start?"

They were not sure, but on the day of the fire Helen had needed to fill the kerosene refrigerator. She recalled that some fuel had spilled on the bark floor as she struggled to pour from the heavy can. Somehow the fumes and the refrigerator flame met.

Now Danis crowded round.

"You won't leave us now, will you?" they pleaded. "We will help you build another house."

"I have brought a small pig for Paul." A Dani placed a piglet in front of the smiling youngster. Everyone knew that was about the finest gift a Dani could give.

Because missionaries from all over the island shared generously of their limited supplies and MAF delivered them for free, the Dekkers soon had necessities. With the help of the Danis, John patched up the washhouse and added a six-foot lean-to for cooking. The family moved into the temporary quarters, but even temporary was too long for Helen. She was pregnant. With the inevitable nausea there was the rain and cold, the mattresses on the bark floor, and bugs and worms dropping through the grass roof. Sometimes she was too sick to cook, but she knew the children didn't suffer. The Danis stuffed them with sweet potatoes and grubs. No one could deny that Paul and Eva were healthy and happy.

John wanted to get the new house up as quickly as possible. Jacques Teeuwen was unable to help because he had developed a serious leg infection. The Danis were willing workers, but they had had no experience in building rectangular structures. In the rush John forgot to put diagonal braces in the center wall, causing it to sag and preventing them from hanging a door on it. He had to figure out a way to prop it up. "This structure is not as sturdy as the fine house our colleagues built for us, but the Danis have never used hammer and nails before. They'll do better next time."

When the Dekkers moved into their new home six

weeks later, they could see that God had turned the fire into a blessing. Funds came from supporters and co-workers. The rough log couch and the crates which had served as tables were replaced by beautiful rattan furnishings bought from Dutch people who had been forced by political pressure to leave the island. Missionary friends had supplied the finishing touches. "Helen has the knack of turning a bush house into a cozy, attractive home," fellow-workers observed after the Dekkers were settled.

Helen and John wrote home, "The whole fire episode has drawn us closer to the Danis. They have seen that we too have problems. They realize that although we have many possessions compared to them, we do not consider the loss of material things too important. Through it all, we were touched and encouraged to see the genuine concern many of the Danis showed for us."

Letters came from friends in the U.S. "We had been praying specifically for you at that time, though we didn't know your problem.

9 Change

In response to the eagerness of Dani youth to hear the gospel, John organized a special program early in 1962. Several times a week, in late afternoon, they gathered in the grass-roofed teaching hut to sing and hear *kiwone*. They were excited about this, because previously only their elders had access to "secret important talk." There were separate groups for girls and boys. Each was divided into five groups according to age, and one was for young marrieds. Each group adopted the name of a man or woman from the Bible and quickly memorized Scripture verses in competition for soccer balls and other prizes.

John would call out, "Romans 6:23."

Someone would recite it.

"*Wa! wa!*" his team members cried.

"John 3:16."

A girl from the *Urut* (Ruth) team recited the verse right through. Some spoke more hesitantly, but all were learning God's Word.

To meet the young people's need for social activities, each group was allowed to plan a feast from time to time. After the meal they played games using balls fashioned from long strips torn from banana stalks and wound round and round into spheres.

Tim—who chose this name when he learned *Timoty* from the Bible—was one of the first in the youth work to become a leader in the literacy program. He went to another village to set up a school, train the teachers, and serve as principal. In May 1962 Judy Eckles, a teacher from America, arrived to coordinate the literacy program, which had spread to every village and hamlet over the hills. While the actual teaching was left to the Danis, Judy supervised. She also took tapes of John's messages out to the villages on weekends, to supplement the teaching of the witness men. The Teeuwens moved to Mamit, a third mission station in the Toli Valley, to work with Frank Clark.

John found it a constant challenge to make the great truths of the Bible relevant in a Stone-Age setting. No cliches would do. Everything he taught had to be soundly based on Scripture. This was a criterion he set for himself because he recalled in his church background restrictions which were not clearly linked to Scripture, such as not buying ice cream or riding public transit on Sundays. These were a problem to him in his youth. He wanted to differentiate between biblical principles and man-made taboos.

He also had to "translate" imagery into what the Danis knew and understood. *How do I explain the Lamb of God who takes away the sin of the world when the Danis have never seen or heard of sheep? First I have to explain the characteristics of sheep, and then tell why Jesus was called the Lamb of God.* Only then could he talk about sacrificing a "piglet," which was familiar to the Danis. Moving from the known to the unknown was always part of the class lesson preparation. Then, in class, he encouraged discussion.

He thought a lot about innovative ways to convey Bible truths. One day to teach the Second Coming of Christ, he cut the heads off half a dozen nails. Next he shaped scrap aluminum to look like nails. A magnet picked up the steel nails but left the aluminum counterfeits. "When Jesus comes, he will take only those who are truly his. Some of you have been listening to God's Word; you've been teaching God's Word; but you have not really become Christians. God knows your hearts."

John cut out little tin and aluminum men. At the next lesson he showed the class how only the tin men were attracted by the magnet. Again he taught, "When Jesus Christ comes again, only true believers (tin men) will go with him. The others (aluminum men) will be left, because even though they look the same as the true believers, they have not been changed in their hearts.

"When Jesus comes, some of you will be caught up, some will be left behind. Jesus is coming soon. It may be today. We must get ready!" A young man, Wabinan, was one who listened. Afterwards he told John, "I am not ready. I want to follow Jesus here and go with him when he comes." From then on he sought God with his whole heart.

Another morning, after the mists and rain had cleared from the hills, John rang the "bell" for class. As he banged a stone on the empty oxygen cylinder he had found in a dump at the coast, the clang reverberated down the valley. None of the men had watches, so the system worked well.

This day as the students arrived at the teaching hut, they were astonished to see John planting weeds out front. Disdainfully they asked, "Why are you planting weeds? We have plenty of them everywhere."

"Just wait. We'll talk about the weeds later," their teacher promised the pupils.

Sin and its roots was the subject. At the appropriate point he began to snip off the weeds flush with the earth. "These weeds represent sins you used to commit. This is stealing. We'll cut it off, seeing you don't steal anymore. This one is lying. We'll cut it off, since you don't lie anymore. This one is war, this one is murder, this one is rape. Now they are all cut off, all gone. Will these plants come up again?" he asked the students.

"Of course they will."

"But they're gone. Why do you say they will come up again?"

"Because the roots are still there."

"Do these sins still have roots in your hearts? Could these sins come into your lives again?" John asked.

"Yes, they could," the Dani agreed.

"What is the main root of sin in your hearts?" John asked. They couldn't answer right away. "Think about it and talk it over while I go to the medical hut for half an hour."

When he returned, one spoke for the group. "We know that our main root of sin is our pride. We Dani men are very proud. We do all sorts of things to show off for the women. At feasts we wear our long ceremonial gourds and swing our hair back and forth to impress the women. We spend much time greasing our long hair in order to draw attention to ourselves." The men talked about pride for some time. Then they prayed together, committing their sin to the Lord.

Later that same day Wuninip and Kininip, another leader, came to John. "Will you please cut our long hair?"

"I can't do that. Why do you want to cut your hair?"

"Tolibaga, remember this morning we identified our pride as our worst root of sin. We feel that our long hair is a symbol of our pride. With it we attract attention to ourselves rather than to God. We must cut our long hair."

"Wait a minute—that's a pretty drastic thing to do in your culture. You'd better pray about it."

"Tolibaga, we have prayed, and we know we must do this."

"Then you must do it yourselves."

"We have no scissors. May we borrow yours?"

Taking the scissors, the men disappeared into the chicken yard, behind the seven-foot fence. Forty-five minutes later they reappeared, looking very self-conscious. Helen was startled. "What happened to Wuninip and Kininip?" John quickly explained. "Wait until the village people see them!"

*   *   *

Wuninip and Kininip set out for the village. Along the way startled Danis asked the same question. "What happened to your hair?" Wide-eyed children scurried ahead to the village to tell their elders.

What will our friends say? Kininip and Wuninip wondered as they walked. Anxiety coursed through Kininip. *Wuninip can return to his house by the Dekkers, but I have to live in the village!* But he didn't regret his action. Each prayed for courage to tell why he had cut his hair. They prayed that the God who had showed them their pride would speak to others too.

When they arrived at the village, the people were watching for them. They crowded around to hear what the two had to say.

"Tolibaga gave us a lesson about the roots of sin in our hearts. He asked us, 'What is the main root of your sin?' We didn't answer right away. He left for a while, and we talked it over. Then we decided that pride is our main sin. Our long hair is what we are most proud of; so we cut it off. God has made us in his likeness that we might show forth his character—not draw attention to ourselves."

Some shook their heads in dismay. Others faintly understood. Some began to examine their own hearts.

In huts throughout the Kanggime area Danis talked about the believers who had cut their long hair. Some were convicted about their lives and motives. Slowly a change came over the Toli Valley. While before only a few had followed the Lord, many were turning to God, realizing what he had done for them in sending his Son.

"It is as if we are living in a different world," John wrote mission staff and supporters. "The atmosphere has completely changed. People have started to love one another. They have confessed their wrongs of the past—stealing, killing pigs, killing persons. They now want to make it right, not only by asking forgiveness, but also by making restitution where possible."

One day Wewo came to the Dekker house. "I want to return something I took."

"Fine. What did you take?"

From his string carrying bag he took something carefully wrapped in leaves. Handing it to John, he emphasized, "This is yours. I took it from the clothesline."

Removing the leafy covering, John saw something black and greasy. "What is this?"

"I used it to carry money in."

After close investigation John determined that it was a baby sock. All color was gone, as well as the original shape. "Thank you very much. I appreciate your returning it."

Smiling as he left, Wewo knew he had done the right thing. Helen and John knew it too, but the sock went into the stove.

Nggembiri appeared at John's office door proudly displaying an old tin can with a wire strung over the top. John recognized it as a "tea billy" he had taken with him on a trek. Not only did the smiling Dani friend return the tin, but he had kept the tea intact without a lid while carrying it over a long, difficult trail.

Now, instead of stealing from the Dekkers or at least trying to get all they could from them, the Danis began to bring gifts—not to obligate them, but to show genuine love and caring. John and Helen were referred to as "friends," and the Danis delighted in calling Helen their "mother" and helping her on the trail.

This caring spirit extended to their neighbors as well as to the Dekkers. The Danis began to understand that those made in the image of God are kind to their neighbor whether he is kind or not. If a neighbor's pig falls into a pit, God's children pick it up. Good turns were no longer to obligate the other person so he would help in return.

"God's children are kind and loving, not for what they can get out of it, but to show the character of God," John reminded his listeners again and again. The Danis were beginning to exhibit the characteristics of their Creator. Kindness, love, goodness, and truthfulness were seen in their lives.

This is becoming a beautiful society, Helen thought as she observed how conscientious and caring the Danis were becoming. Looking toward the mountains she saw the usual rain, but she noticed it less as she contemplated the changing Danis.

When the Danis make even the slightest move toward God, he, like the prodigal's father, runs toward them and pours out his best blessings for them. She was thankful.

Accompanying this turning to God was a desire to be physically clean. "In the past we have been dirty like the pigs. Now that we are God's children, we want to be clean for God." Early in the morning they went to bathe in the cold streams. They wanted the bars of soap the Dekkers previously had tried unsuccessfully to barter for vegetables. "We will work for soap," they said. The men who threw away hairnets caked with pig grease and infested with lice and other vermin wanted soap. The supply quickly ran out.

The Danis' individual need for cleanliness extended to their houses and villages. "We shouldn't have these pigs dirtying things. We shouldn't have the pigs staying in the same hut with our women," the Dani Christians realized. They built clean, new houses for the women and penned the pigs outside the village. Using leaves, they went through the village picking up the pig droppings.

The biggest change was in the attitude of the Dani Christian men toward their wives. The concept of men loving their wives was unknown in Dani society. A Dani husband might be concerned if his wife was sick and grieve if she died, but mostly a woman was a possession. He bought her to work every day in the garden and to live with the pigs. In the past Dani men rarely mentioned their wives because they like to impress others as being free and single. A Dani would be more apt to refer to his wife as a "friend."

Christian men began taking only one wife, and loving her. They talked to their wives with growing respect and cared

for them when they were sick. Many good marriages grew out
of the Dani spiritual awakening.

Instead of the husbands staying in the men's house,
they wanted to live with their wives, "like Wuninip and
Warikwe." Then they could pray together and have family
worship. But soon the wives became pregnant. Often they
were still nursing a baby, and they would lose their milk. With
no milk substitute available, this was a problem. Lacking birth
control methods other than abstinence, the Dani Christian
husbands moved back into the men's house.

A real hunger for the Word of God was another change
in the Danis as a result of the Holy Spirit's work among them.
They built huts near the Dekkers so they could have regular instruction in *kiwone*. While before only a relatively few listened
regularly to the Word of God, now every morning hundreds,
sometimes as many as 2,000, mostly men, came to hear what
God had written in his Book.

"Now that we are God's children, we want to know our
Father," they explained. As they learned more about their
Heavenly Father, the Danis walked to church with a new
dignity. "We are made in the image of our Father, the
Creator. We want to be like him."

As the crowds grew larger, John had the problem of
making them hear. Since there was no public address system,
they had to use relays. John spoke a sentence, then paused
while three or four persons midway in the crowd relayed it to
those at the back. The people gladly listened as long as John
would preach. Since he could not preach all day, he taught the
Danis how to use a tape recorder. After taping his morning
message, he left it with them and attended to other matters,
while they listened hour after hour until they had almost memorized the message.

A second morning Bible class was held at 7:30 for those
with the best spiritual perception. After class these more ad-
vanced students sat with groups on the grass outside, sharing

what they had been taught. On weekends these class members went out two by two to thirteen different preaching points.

In his Bible class for older teenagers, John introduced basic science. And once a week, in an evening class for married couples, he taught birth control, infant care, and basic hygiene.

"Tolibaga, we have been wondering, should God's children be smoking?" the men asked him one morning. "What does God's Word say about this?"

John referred them to the third and sixth chapters of 1 Corinthians. Together they read these Scriptures and talked about their question. "This says my body is the house of the Holy Spirit. I think we are to keep our bodies as healthy as possible and also clean," one suggested. "*Ayee!* Look at the inside of our huts, how black they are from all the smoke. Surely it is not good to make our bodies all black inside." They grimaced.

"We know that if we smoke a lot we get shortwinded on the trails," another reminded them. "We must stop if we want to keep healthy."

Sometimes Dekker walked through the village at night, with an ear to conversations in the little round huts. Almost always talk centered on his lesson of the day, or what God was doing in their midst. Parents were instructing children, with the young people teaching those of their age group who had not been in class.

"I believe this period of change that began with the cutting of the hair is the most important time in the history of the Dani church—more important than the fetish burning which prepared them for this. They are turning to God, being born anew by his Spirit," John reported to the mission.

And so the Dani church grew. But not without problems.

"The way to find the Lord is through waiting on him. You must sit and sing '*Werijo, Werijo.*¹ Then the Spirit of God will enter you," Kelarit, a self-appointed teacher, was telling an up-valley village. And the people, many of them sincere believers, sat in groups on the ground chanting *Werijo* over and over, until some—mostly women—passed out.

"People are finding the Lord and receiving the Holy Spirit when they faint," a Dani reported to the believers at Kanggime.

"What do you think of this?" the Kanggime Christian leaders asked John.

"What do *you* think?" he countered.

"We feel in our spirit it is wrong."

"I agree with you, but perhaps we should wait for awhile."

A week later the Danis learned of a meeting to be held in a village about an hour's walk away. "Shall we go and see for ourselves, Tolibaga?" asked Wuninip and Wabinan. John agreed to accompany them. As they sat in the background and watched, the people chanted, *"Werijo, Werijo, Werijo."* One of the women fell over.

"Ah, she has been born again and now is under the influence of the Holy Spirit," some remarked. Another woman went limp, then another.

"Wuninip, what do you think is really happening?" John asked.

"I don't know, but I don't like it. I think the spirits are making them do this."

John wasn't sure whether it was evil spirits or self-hypnosis. Maybe both. Later John was invited to speak. He told the crowd that he did not believe the chanting was right.

Not long after that, Kelarit held another meeting which John and the Christian Dani leaders attended. The scenario was the same: *"Werijo, Werijo, Werijo,"* and the women fainted. John knew this was wrong.

"Can you bring me some water?" he asked one of the boys standing with him. As soon as he dashed the water on the face of one woman who had passed out, she came to and sat up. Seeing this, the Christian leaders agreed that the chanting and fainting had nothing to do with the Lord, and spoke out against these meetings. Before long the potentially dangerous teaching disappeared.

Others preached what John described as nonsense—meaningless phrases strung together. Some thought that if they did things the way the white people did, their skins would become white. Some who accepted the teaching of *nabelan-kabelan* expected they would live forever physically. When the first Dani believer died, they were perplexed.

John explained, "When you see me walking to the airstrip, you say, 'There is Tolibaga.' At night when you hear me calling out to you, you say, 'There is Tolibaga.' That is different. You don't see me because it is dark, yet you say, 'There is Tolibaga.' You are right. Someday my body will die, and you will see it dead, ready to burn. But that part of me that calls out to you at night will not be there. It will be with the Creator, just as alive as now—more than now, because that part of me will never die."

10 A Church Is Born

At the end of September 1962, John and Helen prepared to go to the coast for the birth of their third child. John asked Wuninip to accompany them so that he could help with translation of study materials while they were there. When Wuninip arrived at the airstrip, he was wearing clothes for the first time. It was also his first plane ride. When the plane hit air pockets, Wuninip reached for something to hold on to. But as he began to relax more, he looked out the window and was excited to see familiar landmarks from a bird's-eye perspective.

"Look, Tolibaga! Isn't that Nop's village?"

"That's it."

"*Ayee!* I've been there too!" he exclaimed as they flew over another village. "And there's the river!"

Soon forgetting his fear, Wuninip thoroughly enjoyed his ride in the *wururu*.

More "firsts" awaited him at the coast. With wonder he eyed the brick houses, cement blocks, and the asphalt roads. "Tolibaga, they don't need to weed these roads, but they are too hard for the pigs to dig for grubs and roots."

He looked at the cars in disbelief. And in the shops he stared and repeated, "All these goods, all these goods!" But most amazing to him was the ocean—"all that salt water!" He stood looking out on the great expanse of water and said to John, "I have gone on long treks to get even a small amount of salt water that dripped out of a mountain, but here—as far as the eye can see—is salt water. Where does it end?"

"It goes on and on. America is that way, Australia that way, Holland the other way," John answered. Wuninip took a bottle of seawater with him to back up the amazing stories he would tell his friends.

Despite the excitement of the "new world," Wuninip went to work. He translated as John completed a book of doctrine based on the Westminister Catechism. They also teamed up on a Scripture-oriented Christian ethics course for teaching Dani believers how they should live with family members and others in society.

In November the Dekkers returned to Kanggime, enriched with a second son, Theo, and eager to implement the much-needed teaching materials. For Wuninip it had been a fruitful trip too. He had helped John with projects that would benefit Dani Christians, and he had grown spiritually doing it.

As Christmas neared, the Danis designated two feast days as part of their observance.

"We need to dig more cooking pits this year for the hundreds of God's children planning to celebrate Christ's birth." Women and children brought in more *mbingga*, corn, and sweet potatoes from the gardens, while the men cut up more pigs. When the time came, John gave a Christmas message while the food cooked. Then they sang. After the feast the Danis presented a tub of pork to the Dekkers, who shared it with the sick villagers. By eight o'clock everyone had returned to their homes.

In one of the village huts a thirteen-year-old boy had returned from the Christmas feast and was thinking about another coming. *Tolibaga has taught us that this same Jesus is coming again.* The prospect so gripped his young heart that he ran out into the village calling, "Listen, everyone! Jesus is coming again!"

Others in the village took up the refrain as they lighted torches and ran toward the airstrip, praising God and singing. As their words were heard in other villages, lines of torch-carrying Danis started streaming over the trails into Kanggime. Night had fallen, and the numerous torches against the black background of the mountains depicted the beautiful drama of living light in a previously dark place. It was a deeply emotional moment for John.

From their house John and Helen watched the swelling crowd gather at one end of the airstrip. The leader shouted, "*Wu! wu! wu! wu!*—as Jesus came in the past, so he is coming again! *Wu! wu! wu! wu!*" The others responded with tumultuous shouts of joy. Then as a group they ran to the other end of the strip, repeating the performance in typical Dani style. The crowds grew as others joined, bringing new torches. Up and down the airstrip, singing and chanting, they surged.

"I wonder what prompted this demonstration?" John decided to find out. "Who started this?" John asked one of the Danis.

"Muta, your houseboy!"

John looked for the youngster. "Muta, what is this all about?"

"Tolibaga, I was thinking how wonderful it was that God came to live among us, but what we've been celebrating today took place a long time ago. You have taught us that Jesus is coming again. This is more exciting than the feast of Christmas! He might come any day—we must be ready!"

Walking back to the house, John turned and looked at the Dani Christians with their torches of joy. He felt the Lord must be pleased.

"Tolibaga, should we not be baptized?"

John and other missionaries to the Danis had discussed the matter of baptism. In view of the Danis' propensity for making group decisions, the missionaries agreed to delay. They did not want the Danis to perceive baptism as a talisman to bring them good things. John had been reluctant to baptize any converts until he could ground them in the essentials of the Christian faith. Now that he had the Dani catechism and the Christian ethics course, he arranged baptism readiness courses for the leaders who had proven themselves.

In February 1963 thousands witnessed the first baptism in the Toli Valley. John planted an eight-foot cross near the baptismal pool. "Kanggime is no longer 'The Place Where You Die.' Because you believe that Christ died for your sins, you have new life. Now as you go down into the water, you proclaim that you are dead to your old desires and alive to Christ."

Wuninip was the first to step into the pool. "I baptize you in the name of the Father, the Son, and the Holy Spirit." Twelve other Dani leaders followed. "Now that we have a church, it must have elders," John announced. He appointed Wuninip and Tekola. Like Wuninip, Tekola had keen perception in things of the Lord. Although older than the other students, he had learned to read and write quickly. He was an encouragement to the Danis.

Then they gathered at the foot of the cross for the first Communion service, while others watched. After John took the bread—a cold, cooked sweet potato—and broke it into bite-size pieces, he placed it on a banana leaf and passed it to those who had been baptized. He then took the wine—wild red raspberry juice in bamboo containers—and passed it among the thirteen.

In response to the Danis' request to use the Dekkers' blue plastic pitcher for Communion wine, John told them, "You should use your own water gourds." He was thinking to keep it a Dani-type service, but the Danis could not understand his reasoning. "Why won't you share your things with us?" they asked in disappointment. "We want the best for remembering the Lord." They compromised on the bamboo containers.

John opened the service with a reminder. "It is only

because of what Jesus accomplished on the cross that we can have communion with God."

Then Tekola prayed. "O you who are our Creator, greetings. You have come into our world and made yourself known to us through Tolibaga. Greetings! Thank you for the forgiveness of our sins. Thank you for the new life which you have given us. Thank you for bringing peace in our valley."

During the next five months 150 Danis were baptized. As the young church took shape, it became evident that God had given many special gifts to strengthen it. Wuninip had the gift of pastoral work, others that of teaching or evangelism. Others carried on spiritual oversight or helped the sick and needy. The new church formally recognized these gifts by appointing deacons and two more elders, Nonit and Wimili, both members of the first witness class. The leaders also drew up a service for the dedication of believers' children. This was only two and a half years after the Kanggime Danis first encountered Christian missionaries.

John now remembered how he had prayed for the Danis as he and Helen flew back to Kanggime from the coast the year before. He was beginning to see the prayer answered.

One of the first matters the young church had to deal with was the bride price, usually paid in pigs. Traditionally the Danis spent much time haggling over the amount to pay for a bride, and then making the payments. "Let's be done with it," many Dani Christians said. "The bride price is the cause of most of our disagreements. It has even led to wars and killing."

"But the bride price is deeply ingrained in your economy. You can't just throw it out," John remonstrated. He had talked about it with missionaries involved with Dani believers in other areas, and they had come to the same conclusion.

The Dani elders argued, "Too many payments, Tolibaga!" They went on to remind him of the Dani tradition. "The husband-to-be has to make the first payment to the bride's family. Then the bride's father and his relatives make one to the bride's mother and her kin. And that's not all. The husband has to continue to make payments, sometimes years after the marriage! If the pigs are too small, there can be trouble, even fighting.

"Tolibaga, as people of God we don't want fighting anymore. We don't need this trouble. We don't want this trouble. We want to end bride payments. You say it may disrupt our economy, but even that is better than fighting. We think that marriage should be on the basis of mutual love and family consent."

"Couldn't you agree on a one-time payment that would not be excessive?" John and other missionaries suggested. Even though government officials made it known they were not in favor of abolishing the bride price, the church was adamant.

On another day the elders discussed with John the matter of courtship gatherings. They questioned whether God's children should be involved in these traditional Dani get-acquainted socials, which began with eligible young men and women exchanging armbands with the partners of their choice and usually ended with sexual relations.

"What does the Scripture say? Let's turn to *kiwone*." As they studied the passages on fornication, the Holy Spirit convicted the Danis, and the church ruled out the practice for all believers. Even outside the church, the Dani society's penalty for adultery was to tie up the man and make him pay up to three or four pigs—a heavy fine in Daniland. If he was caught again, he could be beaten and banished from society for awhile. Incest was punishable by death.

After the Dani church abandoned the courtship rites, the elders decided they should establish a Christian way. The women would still propose, and many decided to send a note to the man via a friend. One of the witness men brought such a note to John. The woman had written: "While I was praying, the Lord impressed me that you are to be my husband."

"What shall I do, Tolibaga?"

"Has God told you that you are to be her husband?"

"No, he has not."

"If, after you pray about it, you really feel she is the one God wants you to marry, then marry her. But don't let this note alone decide for you."

"But it is written down, Tolibaga . . ."

"You pray," John insisted. The wedding never took place.

Other times, if a man was pleased with the proposal he talked with his parents first, and if they agreed he talked with her parents. Then the young man approached the Dani pastor. If he agreed to the marriage, the date was set. At the outdoors service in the afternoon, the husband's people would sit on one side, the bride's on the other. The bride and groom stand before the pastor, she wearing a new skirt and he his best gourd. His hair is trimmed neatly. It is a solemn time as the couple stands before the minister, never looking at each other. After they are pronounced man and wife, he goes back to his people, and she walks a few steps behind with eyes downcast.

A pig feast follows, with chickens and lots of sweet potatoes and *mbingga*. The women snack on the delicacy of the pigs' intestines and the eyes, while the children toss the pigs' bladders around like toy balloons. They all sing and laugh and wish the bride and groom well. Toward evening the newlyweds slip away to his mother's hut or to their own.

In the days of intertribal fighting, there was no desire for communication among the villages. Since peace had come to the valley, it was different. "Now that we are one big family, let's make good paths so we can visit one another," the Christians suggested.

The only trails the Danis had made were from the villages to their gardens. If they trekked beyond this, they followed single file on paths beat down by the pigs. These were often out-of-the-way, much longer routes than they needed to be. The Christians wanted trails where two or three people could walk together, and they wanted them to be more direct. John welcomed the idea. Such improvements would cut down the time it took him to go to the thirteen preaching points which he visited regularly. The closest was now a thirty-minute fast hike; the most distant took half a day. And the gospel was reaching into new villages even farther afield. John sometimes walked all day to reach Karubaga when the missionary aircraft could not get in to Kanggime due to bad weather or if he had needs that could not wait for the scheduled plane.

"If we could get a powerful motorbike that would climb these mountains," John speculated, "I could spend less time on the trail and more time ministering to the people."

Still, trekking through the forest was an experience he thoroughly enjoyed. On one occasion the Danis pointed out the rare yellow birds of paradise with their long plumage, and such interesting varieties of foliage as the large Guinea tree with its white trunk and lacy green leaves which fold up at night, spiky palms, long and short needled pines, and thick tropical philodendron with huge showy leaves. Small flowers of every color line the paths and hug the little springs. Tiny pale green orchids cling to the hillsides.

Could we build a road good enough for a motorbike to travel through this forest and over these mountains? John wondered. *If we're going to improve the trails and make them wider, why not do it right.*

A motor road from Kanggime to Karubaga was most needed, John decided. This could be a project for Costas Macris who had just arrived from Greece with his wife, Alky, and baby Jonathan to take over the station while John and Helen went on furlough. *Costas can learn the language while he works with the Danis on the road.* He would also supervise the medical work.

As further preparation for going on furlough in June

1963, Wuninip was ordained the first pastor of the Kanggime church. He was the most respected leader among the Danis, one of the first men in the witness school, the first to cut his hair, and the first to be baptized in the Toli Valley. He was a perceptive Christian, responsive in witness class, able to quickly memorize Scripture, and to relate deep truth to the Dani culture. He was God's man for the task. Warikwe, his wife, also was a good influence in the community.

While the Dani elders and RBMU personnel placed their hands on his head, church members stretched out their hands toward Wuninip, and John offered the ordination prayer.

Wuninip realized his new responsibility as spiritual leader. "Tolibaga won't be here. O Creator God, help me!"

When the Dekkers left on their first furlough, it was with the assurance that God had provided people who would nurture the various ministries at Kanggime. He had brought Costas and Alky from Europe, and Judy from North America. He had filled Wuninip's searching heart, and would undergird him as he pastored his people.

In the plane Helen's and John's thoughts turned to their "leave of absence from duty," as the dictionary defines furlough. It wouldn't be that totally. Each had ambitious "priority projects" lined up for their North America visit. Along with these, they anticipated seeing friends, relatives, and supporters—those who had faithfully interceded, not always knowing the desperate circumstances of the ones they remembered.

Far removed from North American faithful, John's parents in Holland also had prayed. On their way to North America the Dekkers stopped off in Holland to share with John's relatives what God had done among the Danis and to show the children to his parents. Though the parents gave the family a warm, hospitable welcome, John knew they regretted seeing so little of their grandchildren. But his parents kept the usual tight rein on their emotions, happy that their son was in the Lord's work.

John thought about the young man who had left Holland nearly a decade before in search of the "more to life" he felt there must be. He had found it.

In Canada and the United States they discovered unknown prayer supporters from many denominations. "We have been praying for you every day," they heard frequently.

"We're glad, but why didn't you write and tell us? At times we were very aware that somebody was holding us up before the Throne, but we didn't know who. If you would write or send a Christmas card saying, 'I'm praying for you,' it would be an encouragement."

In Toronto at The Peoples Church, which had supported them from the start, the Dekkers were moved to learn that the well-informed women's missionary prayer group had kept up with the lives and needs of the Dekkers and the Danis. "Did the children get over the impetigo? How is Eva's ear? Does she have any hearing loss? How is your new house? Tell us about Wuninip, we've prayed so much for him."

"We can't tell you how encouraged we are to hear that you used our prayer letters to pray so specifically for our needs. To find that you still remember details of the work is the greatest encouragement of our furlough," Helen told them.

Discouragement came too—in a tape from Wuninip.

"Dear Tolibaga: We are having much sickness, and many are dying because there are no medicines. Some of the weaker Christians are afraid that ancestral spirits are bringing revenge. They are turning back to the old witchcraft ways. One even became involved in an offering to ancestral spirits."

Quickly John worked to meet their desperate need. He contacted drug companies for supplies of free or low-cost

medications, and raised funds to cover shipping them. Soon he
was able to write to Wuninip and Costas: "Good news—a drug
shipment is coming. Also a supporter has given us a motorbike.
Tell the brethren to keep up the good work on the roads. A
Harley-Davidson is on the way!"

Then he turned to one of his furlough projects—looking
into Bible study materials for the Dani pastors. He wanted to
put together a one-year program that would cover a survey of
the Old Testament, the life of Christ, and basic doctrines.
With such an arrangement, a pastor receiving only one year of
instruction would be exposed to some of each category.
Second- and third-year programs would enlarge on the teach-
ings of Christ and present doctrines in more detail.

Helen too had been gathering supplies to take back.
John didn't know she was secretly hoping that the Lord would
tell them to stay home. Even on furlough she had to deal with
memories of isolation and the fear of not measuring up to what
a missionary should be. No such change of orders came
through. *Reluctant though I am to return, I know it is what
you want me to do,* Helen prayed.

The Dani Christians, Judy Eckles, and the Macrises
gathered at the airstrip in March 1964, waiting for the MAF
plane. Wuninip led in prayer: "Lord, you know how much we
have longed for them to be back among us, but you know that
we are not looking to our dear friend, Tolibaga, but to you
alone."

As they waited, Judy remembered a day before Costas
had come to Kanggime when she had asked John, "Don't you
miss having another man to talk to?" Quickly John had replied, "I have Wuninip, and he is my friend." John was not
only a father figure to the Danis, but he was a friend who
walked with them and taught them, Judy had observed. John
gave himself to them without limitations. Too much so, some
of the other missionaries thought, and had chided him for his

insensitivity to the needs of his own family. *Yet, John's spirit of oneness with the Dani Christians—could this be one reason such strong Christians have developed among the Danis?*

Her musings ended. The plane had landed.

"Costas should have been a landscape architect!" the Dekkers exclaimed when they saw what he and the Danis had accomplished in such a short time. An amphitheatre was ready to seat the increasing number of Danis waiting to hear *kiwone*. Around the clinic and the Dekker's house, decorative stone walls enhanced the setting. Tiny orchids, orange lilies, and rhododendrons spilled over flower beds. Lantana bushes attracted iridescent turquoise butterflies. "Wherever Costas goes, he creates beauty," Helen observed.

"And he gets the more difficult jobs done too," John noted as he heard that the road to Karubaga was nearly complete. "How did you do it?" John asked, visualizing—as he had many times while he was away—the cuts through rock and the deep gorges that had to be bridged.

"The Danis with their digging sticks, steel axes, and shovels are a productive team," Costas replied. "Hundreds of Danis worked at it. As much as possible, we routed the road around the hills rather than over them."

"And the bridge over the main gorge?"

"It's twenty-five feet long and five feet wide. The approaches to it were difficult because they had to turn sharply from the mountain. But the Danis broke through the mountain rock like nothing!"

John knew it had been an ambitious project, with no machinery—only a combination of Stone-Age and twentieth-century hand tools. He was grateful for the Danis' perseverence, and the expert direction of Costas.

Then they saw the new school with hand-hewn desks where the Danis could learn to write as well as to read. The Dekkers heard that the work of the church had prospered under Wuninip. Instead of thirteen preaching points, twenty-four groups were now meeting. And the youth work had grown.

"What happened here?" John asked several Danis as they walked along the plateau. Instead of fishponds he saw only muddy depressions. "Where is the water—and the fish?"

"Ah, Tolibaga, we hunted all the big fish. Then some of the people were hungry for the little fish. When they could not get the fish out of the water, they made a way for the water to come out of the pond. We ate the little fish, and now there are no more," they sheepishly admitted. It wasn't long before the youth groups volunteered to look after the project—if Tolibaga would help them restock the ponds. The plan worked so well it was soon picked up in other villages, and fish became a favorite food.

11 A Growing Church

"Your motorcycle has arrived at the coast," John heard on the radio-phone.

"Great, send it in," he instructed the MAF.

"No, you'll have to come to see it first."

"That's a waste of time. Just send it."

But the MAF pilots were adamant. So John took Muta and flew to the coast.

"Hey, that's a big one," John exclaimed when he saw the 900-pound Harley-Davidson, complete with sidecar. "I've never ridden a motorcycle—never liked the things." He looked it over. "Here's the brake, and this must be the clutch."

"Okay, Muta, let's give it a try."

Muta got on behind Tolibaga while the MAF pilots watched.

Slowly, uncertainly John started. The bike wobbled.

"More speed should help," John hit the accelerator. *Less wobble, but too much power!* He struggled to balance and control the heavy machine. Five hundred yards down the stretch the machine won. They were in the ditch.

"I'm going to try again, Muta."

"Tolibaga, if we die, we'll die together and go to Heaven!"

They ditched again.

John recognized the true nature of the "beast." He couldn't tame it.

"Even if I learn to drive this, it will never do on the mountain trails."

Resigned driver and relieved passenger pushed the bike back to the hangar.

"Please give me a piece of cardboard," John asked the pilots. With felt pen he lettered "For Sale" and hung it on the Harley-Davidson.

The pilots laughed. "That's what we hoped you would do. When we saw the size of the motorcycle, we were afraid you would kill yourself on the narrow trails.

Not long afterwards John received a call.

"The bike is sold."

"Good. Now Dave Martin and I can order a DOT motorbike from England. They are powerful hill-climbers with big knobby tires to claw over rough terrain, yet light enough to walk them through a landslide," he told the pilots. "And the Villiers engine parts are available in Australia."

"When it arrives, we'll call you!"

Since returning from furlough John's top priority was preparing the Christian leadership training materials for the twenty men serving as pastors. This needed to be printed—not only for the Leadership Training School he planned, but so there would be copies in case the Dekkers and the other missionaries were forced for political or other reasons to leave. Having Bible study materials in print would also help if Satan tried to confuse the Danis in these matters.

A tremendous amount of work was involved. Although some parts of the Bible had been translated into Dani by Dave Scovill of UFM and Gordon Larson of C & MA, almost all of the lesson material and much of the accompanying Scripture had to be translated. This meant many long hours with Wuni-nip and other language informants. John typed the masters and ran off copies on the small duplicator, then stapled them into books. Aggravating problems slowed the work. The carbon paper became hard, resulting in poor copies, and the old hand-crank duplicator often didn't work without coaxing. John got hold of some slides to illustrate such Old Testament stories as Jonah and the big fish, the tabernacle, and other subject matter which was totally outside the Dani experience or imagining.

John was spending at least four afternoons each week, plus a couple of hours most evenings in this lesson preparation. One evening Helen tried repeatedly to get his attention. Finally, in exasperation she calmly shoved the typewriter off the table onto the floor. John grinned at her in astonishment.

"John, you do have a family. You must spend some time with us." Paul and Eva and even little Theo loved to climb onto their daddy's lap for a bedtime story. John tried to make himself available, but sometimes the pressure of work interfered.

While John worked on the leadership materials, the Dani pastors decided they needed to develop a form of church organization that would be recognized by the government, and through which they could deal with the government in solidarity. John did not want to impose any particular form of organization on the young church.

"Why don't we look at what we have right here," he suggested. What they saw was a group of local churches, each with its own pastor. Also there were senior pastors who were looked up to by the others and who were often called on for advice by a number of churches. Thus the idea of a Kanggime Church Council came into being quite naturally. It was made up of five leading pastors chosen by the churches to represent the twenty-four congregations meeting regularly in the area. These mature men gave counsel and ruled in cases where arbitration was necessary. The other Toli Valley churches in Karubaga and Mamit areas developed church councils in the same way, and from time to time the three councils met together to discuss problems they were experiencing. If a pastor came to John with a problem, John asked, "Have you seen your Council member?" He involved himself only with matters on the council level.

He met with the Kanggime Council each Friday morning to pray and to discuss church problems, which were varied. Some pastors wanted to share the pulpit all the time. John advised them to do this only once a month. "Otherwise your people might not be taught the whole Word of God, or some topics might be missed. You need system in your teaching."

They brought up another problem. "Tolibaga, as you know, for some time our people have been walking to church on Sundays in single file, very quietly, talking only in whispers. Now they are scolding a child who stops to pull a blade of grass. 'You cannot pick anything green on Sunday!' they say. Are they doing right?"

"What do you think? This walking in whispers—is it a holy hush from the Spirit of God? Is this idea of not picking anything green from *kiwone*, or is it like one of the old taboos? When you embraced Christianity, you put aside the old taboos. When God gave Adam and Eve the Sabbath, it was not to keep them from doing this or that, but to keep it as a special day for God—a day to think about God, to worship him. Let's not start taboos."

A major problem was how to provide activities to take the place of the old celebrations and festivals the Danis gave up when they became Christians. "When we stopped making war, we also stopped all the exciting activity that went with it. Practicing for war was exciting; so was the dressing up, and the celebration after victory. We don't have the bride price feasts, courtship gatherings, and dancing feasts anymore. Our people are missing these social times. We need more occasions to get together, to feast, to play and to be joyous."

They introduced sports days, featuring contests and games. The Danis had learned to play soccer, but it required a sizable piece of cleared ground. Volleyball worked well in a small area, while wheelbarrow and sack races provided action and laughs. All helped to meet the Danis' social needs.

While the Dani church dealt with its growing pains, Helen and John went to the coast to welcome their fourth child. Daniel David, born in October, was Eva's third brother.

While John was on furlough, no Danis were baptized at Kanggime. Many had asked for baptism, but the Dani church leaders were not anxious to do the questioning involved to eliminate those who saw baptism as a kind of initiation rite into the church. The leaders preferred that John be the one to say "no" rather than having to face community pressure themselves. In some cases John had to refuse important members of the community. Though they had the right answers, they were not wholeheartedly following the Lord.

After interviewing many who had asked for baptism, John agreed to baptize 140 believers. The service was scheduled for a Sunday in December, but people from outlying villages began to arrive on Friday. Helen saw Kanggime Christians carrying bananas, sugarcane, nuts, and other foods, singing and chanting as they walked. "What are they doing?" she asked Leleki.

"God's children in Kanggime are giving food to the visiting Danis," Leleki explained.

It was a simple thing, but Helen's heart was touched to see that the Danis' relationship with God was such that he could guide them into acts of love. No one had suggested that the Kanggime Christians do this. After they had finished singing, they ran down the airstrip and presented their gifts in an orderly way. Then they explained to the visitors where they would sleep during their stay in Kanggime.

On Sunday thousands witnessed the baptisms and heard testimonies.

John also assisted with a baptism in the village of Bogot-

nuk, about an hour's walk from Kanggime. A man who was
fairly old by Dani standards and who had been blind for many
years was led into the pool, while about 3,000 watched.

"Nigitpaga, in the name of the Father and the Son and
the Holy Spirit, I baptize you." John lowered him into the
water, then helped him back to his friends who took him to
shore. As John continued with the service, he was aware of
some commotion on the bank. Afterward he asked the Dani
pastor what happened.

"Tolibaga, God has done a wonderful thing—Nigitpaga can see! It happened as he came out of the water."

John went over to the old man, who by now was the
center of great rejoicing. "I have heard of 'white men,' but
now I see you. Praise God!"

Persons with severe illnesses that usually resulted in
death were prayed for and were restored to health. The Dani
Christians accepted the truth of *kiwone* with total, childlike
trust in their newfound Father. They came to God with their
requests, expecting him to answer. And he did. One night a
boy wakened John crying, "My brother has gone crazy! He is
stumbling around saying crazy things, and he's very hot."

John hurried toward the man's hut, praying for help in
diagnosis as he went. *High fever, delirious—cerebral malaria!
The man could be dead in six hours!* John backtracked to his
house for antimalarial pills. He crushed them, and while
others held the frenzied man, John forced him to swallow the
medicine. As they continued to hold him they prayed, committing him to the Lord. *More than medicine is needed for this
one.* By morning the man was still weak, but the fever was
gone and he was lucid. He recovered completely.

Another living testimony of God's healing in the early
days of the Kanggime church was Kuwa, a Dani woman.
Though there had been no major intertribal fighting since
1960, occasional minor skirmishes broke out. Kuwa was working in her garden near Paba where there had been fighting between two groups. "Let's get them in their gardens," one group
said, and Kuwa was shot full of arrows. She appeared to be

dead when, later in the day, she was carried into the village. For weeks she remained barely alive, unconscious most of the time. In her conscious moments she was told of God's love and way of salvation, and she believed. Though she was very sick, she wanted to be baptized. After her baptism, the many arrowheads that had broken off and were embedded in her body, causing infection, dissolved—something the Danis had never seen before.

By 1965 twenty churches were flourishing as a result of the RBMU Kanggime outreach, and as many in both the Karubaga and Mamit districts. As estimated 20,000 lived in the areas served by the three mission bases located in the Toli Valley.

At that year's Karubaga conference of the RBMU's thirty-five missionaries, all agreed that the Christian Leadership Training School at Kanggime was a success. "Why not move it to Karubaga?" a delegate suggested. "It would be more centrally located for all the Dani believers in the area."

Leave Kanggime! Because the very thought pained John, he was soon vigorously opposing the idea. "I know all the people of Kanggime and I love them."

"The hospital and government post are here."

"And planes can land here most any time, whereas Kanggime is often weathered in." Arguments in favor of the move were spilling forth.

"Logical arguments I know," John conceded, "but leaving the people of Kanggime would be like leaving family!"

"You can go back and forth," the others suggested. "Perhaps weekend supervision is all Kanggime needs now. When the DeLeeuws come back from furlough, Bruno can help strengthen the church and Marlys can supervise the medical work."

John still objected, but he was overruled.

Despite the great disappointment, once the decision was made his response was, "Let's get on with it." He wrote to supporters: "The Lord has overwhelmingly answered our prayers for the Danis. Many thousands have been born into the family of God. We now have to give absolute priority to training the Dani church leaders. What we are planning will cost about $4000 and although we do not have these funds now, we feel that we must go ahead so that we can start our school year on schedule."

John went to Karubaga and the DeLeeuws came to Kanggime.

The only site large enough to accommodate the school buildings and student huts was a swampy area on the plateau about a half mile from Karubaga. "Would people living there be willing to relocate for the school?" When John explained that they would be reimbursed for their move, they were agreeable. He also persuaded local people to give garden space to the students so that they could grow their own food.

Thousands of Danis came from Toli Valley churches to help build the Sekolah Alkitap Maranata (SAM), Indonesian for Maranatha Bible School. It was a major construction undertaking that had not been part of the Dani experience or even their imagination. But the Danis were hard workers and teachable. After they were divided into crews to do specific jobs, the work was explained to them. Then, while one crew cleared the brush from the construction site and laid stone drainage ditches, other Danis went into the high forest to cut trees. They stripped the bark and cut the timber into lengths of six to nine feet. Then they split the wood and with stone adzes neatly chiseled boards ranging in size from 1" x 8" to 1" x 12". At the construction site the builders overlapped the boards slightly to keep out the strong winds. By mid-August two classrooms were ready and the chapel was almost completed. They still had to build three more school buildings and two missionary homes, one for Judy Eckles and another for the Dekkers.

The Bible school students were to build their own huts in three student villages of approximately thirty-five each. In addition to twenty-five for living, one was planned as a cooking hut to be shared by five families, another for giving birth, and a couple to house those who became ill with infectious diseases such as pneumonia, dysentery, malaria, or colds.

John laid out the village carefully. To keep the huts evenly spaced, he drove in stakes at intervals of twenty-four feet to mark the center of each ten-foot hut. With a five-foot length of rope attached to the stake, he outlined the circular area.

Meanwhile, in the villages elders prayerfully went through the long lists of potential candidates for the new Bible school and selected thirty men who had already proven themselves in the work of the Lord. Many had expressed a desire to attend, but only nine from each of the three mission areas could go the first year. In each area the candidates were screened by the literacy supervisor, who narrowed the number to ten or twelve. The names of the finalists were returned to the local church elders, who sought the Holy Spirit's guidance in selecting nine. Most of the men chosen had come up through the youth program. It was important that the man's wife also have a good testimony and that she attend classes, though on a less rigorous schedule because of having children to care for.

On the choice of Bitbet the elders were unanimous. "We want Bitbet to go for sure. He is outstanding." A literacy teacher and youth leader in his church in the village of Egoni across the valley from Kanggime, Bitbet had also been a keen student in the Christian Leadership program the year before in Kanggime. His wife, Worop, also was outstanding. Bitbet was one of the first students to arrive at Karubaga to build his hut. Over the trails he and his wife, Worop, and their little child traveled, carrying their few belongings. Several friends, balancing five-foot boards on their shoulders, accompanied them. At the homesite, Bitbet and his helpers lashed the uprights together with forest vines and gathered fresh green grass to thatch the roof which would soon burn brown from the sun. For flooring they placed poles across the hut and covered them with large sheets of bark. Bitbet then divided his snug little house into three sections like pieces of a pie: one wedge was a bedroom for Bitbet, his wife, and baby. Another was the living area with an enclosed nook for Bitbet's desk and books. The remainder was for the young girl who had come to baby-sit their child while they were in classes. She was a relative of Bitbet's; only girls from the husband's family were permitted to share family quarters. No fires were allowed in the huts, but the school provided blankets. Their house finished, they turned to preparing the garden they hoped would furnish them with food while they went to school.

Helen was delighted with the move to Karubaga. The larger community with its medical and government facilities helped counteract the feeling of isolation that had continued to be a problem to her at Kanggime. She welcomed being nearer medical help for the children. Muta and Leleki, their faithful household helpers who had become like family members, had moved to Karubaga too. Just before leaving Kanggime they had been married.

From the Dekker home the view of the mountain ranges was spectacular and the house itself, made of hand-hewn boards, was attractive. Purple and red bougainvillea accented the entrance, and a stream ran through the back garden. There was one problem. *If only we didn't have all these bugs!* was Helen's daily refrain. Despite an aluminum roof on the house, the pesky beetles got in under it and dropped through the woven reed ceiling onto the floor, table, and bed. Each morning Helen swept, only to see more beetles drop.

Learning of this, a women's group in Montana took up a special offering. "This $700 is to fix a proper bedroom for Helen," they wrote. John was able to buy enough hardboard to completely line their room (ceiling and walls) to keep out the insect hordes. Helen's mother gave money to purchase pretty yellow wallpaper, bedspread, and draperies. The room pro-

vided a relaxed haven for Helen and John in the heavily
scheduled days when Helen too was teaching at the school.

Little Paul, not quite six years old, left for the C & MA
Missionary Boarding School at Santani. The four and a half
month separation sounded like forever to Helen who prayed,
"Please, Lord, look after our little boy." She tried to put a
weekly treat on the MAF plane out to the coast—oranges, tan-
gerines, sweet potatoes, or peanuts—for the little boy who
thought, *I will never see my mommy or daddy again.*

Bitbet and Worop got up at sunrise. Carrying towels
the school had issued, and soap, they walked to the cold river
for their daily bath. The women went upstream, while the
men used an area around the bend. Then, as the sun filtered
through the mountain mist, they returned to their home.
Breakfast was usually leftover sweet potatoes which they ate
cold or warmed. Sometimes they roasted fresh ones. While
Worop attended to the baby, Bitbet sat on a little two-legged
stool in front of the hut and studied. When he and Worop
heard the clang of the old fire extinguisher, about 8:30, they
walked to chapel. They spent all morning and an hour in the
afternoon in classes.

Darkness came early in the highlands, making classroom lights necessary. A diesel generator was switched on
about 6:00 P.M. and supplied power to provide lights in the
classrooms for extra study time. In their own huts the students
had only small kerosene lamps fashioned from empty tin cans
or bottles. Most evenings Bitbet and Worop studied in the
lighted classroom, while the baby-sitter cared for the children.
Between 9:30 and 10 John shut off the generator, and it was
lights out.

Women attended separate classes where they could
have babies under two years old with them for breast-feeding.
Helen also gave Bible school mothers special tickets to the
clinic. These entitled them to service without a wait when the

babies were sick and enabled them to return to class more quickly. It was not easy for young mothers to keep their minds on lessons with babies to care for. Nor was it easy for the teacher as she competed with babies for their mothers' attention.

In 1966, after Paul went away to school, Helen started teaching a women's class. At the beginning many of the women who enrolled in the first year Life of Christ course could not read. Helen, who was teaching in Dani for the first time, sometimes stumbled along with her students learning to read. She constantly encouraged them to *think* about what they read. They were quick to memorize, but she would say, "Tell me in your own words what you read. What does it mean?" she would ask over and over. She stressed that in reading God's Word they should listen to the Holy Spirit as he made it clear to them. By the end of the first year she was gratified to see them applying God's Word in their lives. Later women Bible school students were required to pass a reading and Scripture-finding entrance exam, and the course was extended to three years.

Women students sometimes had problems with the young baby-sitters who cared for the older children. These girls were not always skilled or careful, resulting in several children being injured. Other hurdles women students had to overcome were their own shyness and the low opinion many had of themselves. "You can do it," Helen encouraged. The idea that women could learn was new to them. Actually many did as well as the men. In addition to going with the men on weekends, preaching and teaching, they developed their own ministries.

Sometimes during the three-year program the students didn't have enough food. "Tolibaga, you didn't tell us how difficult it would be for us to get food," Bitbet chided one day. There were times during the year when there were not enough potatoes. "Why don't you stagger plantings," John urged Bitbet and other students. This helped assure a continuing supply, but they couldn't plant in the rainy season or at the height of the dry season. Churches which sent students to school were supposed to supplement their food when necessary, but sometimes failed to do this. Relatives occasionally walked three to six hours to bring food for the struggling students.

John was concerned about their need, but felt that to dole out food might be only a stopgap. The Danis had to learn to solve problems, to be resourceful, and to look to the Lord. A student testified in class: "One night I was very hungry for sweet potatoes and greens. Then I remembered that God said in *kiwone* that if we seek his kingdom first, he will supply our food and other needs (Matthew 6:33). I prayed, and the next day God gave me potatoes and greens."

God showed himself wonderfully powerful in other ways. One young couple, Bani and Nggebu Bembok, had wanted children for a long time. Shortly after one of the Christians laid hands on them and prayed, Bani conceived and bore a child.

Tamyri, another of the Bible school women, developed a large running sore at the base of her throat. Since no antibiotics were effective, the doctor was sure it was cancer of the thyroid. John explained to her husband, Neenit, that unless God intervened, his wife had only a short time to live and she should prepare to meet the Lord. "He will make it well, Tolibaga," Neenit replied without hesitation. And so they prayed for her "with a strong faith in their hearts."

On a stretcher they carried Tamyri from the hospital back to her little hut where she continued to nurse her baby. Her condition worsened until the skin was stretched tight over her bones, except for her grotesquely swollen legs. Tamyri remained cheerful, totally trusting God, and Neenit tenderly cared for his sick wife.

Each day Helen stopped by the little hut with soup or other food, and occasionally gave Tamyri a vitamin B-12 injection "just to make her feel a little better." Every day Tamyri was smiling and praising God. Often during the visits she said,

"*Ala an ñogoba, nano?* (God is my Father, can't you understand that? Of course he's going to heal me!)."

As Helen walked home from one of these visits, marvel-
ing at Tamyri's faith, she prayed, "God you wouldn't dare *not*
heal that woman!"

At Helen's next visit Tamyri looked so much better. The
swelling in her legs was going down, the lumps and running
sores gradually disappeared, and she began to put on weight.
When the new school term commenced, Tamyri was in class.
Helen sent her back to the doctor for an examination.

"I hardly recognize this woman," Dr. Elizabeth Cous-
ens wrote back to Helen. "All symptoms of her previous condition have gone, and her general health is now very good.
Her recovery from severe illness is unquestionable." To which
God's children said, "Praise God!"

In Helen's Bible class one morning a young mother
stood up and praised God for giving her baby back to her. "My
baby was sick and died in the night. Next morning as the men
prepared the funeral pyre, I was cradling my dead baby in my
arms when I remembered the lesson you had taught us about
the widow of Nain. Jesus is the same today, I thought, so I
prayed, 'God, you gave that widow's child back to her. You
can do the same for me.' Then my baby began to breathe!"[1]
The class rejoiced and praised God.

And out in the villages the Christians thanked God for
healings too. Mbowan Weyanggurik had injured his leg behind
the knee, resulting in serious infection. Because he had kept his
leg bent to favor it, the flesh had grown together, joining the
upper and lower leg. To get around he hopped with a stick.
Then he became a Christian and was baptized. The elders
prayed, and in a matter of a week he could straighten his leg
and walk without the stick. He walked normally among the
people, a living testimony to the Lord's power.

When Woranip, who was born a deaf mute, "heard"
the gospel through sign language, he became a Christian and

was baptized. Afterward the Lord gradually restored his hearing, and enabled him to learn to speak.

Worenikwe had been blind for many years. She heard the gospel and believed. After she was baptized and prayed for by the elders, her sight was totally restored. She threw away her walking stick and went back to work in her garden.

At the Bible school, classes ended at 11 A.M. on Fridays so students who wished to return to their villages could do so. Every Friday John was on his bike with a Dani riding behind, headed for Kanggime. The mountain road was treacherous, particularly in the rainy season when landslides sometimes blocked passages and bikers had to make temporary tracks on the side of the mountain to get through. Where bridges were washed away, they would throw a few slippery poles across the stream and do a balancing act to the other side. If the stream was wide, they got together a group of Danis who with whooping and hollering carried the bike, suspended from a long pole, across the stream.

Even in the best times, parts of the road took real courage to negotiate. Downhill on steep slopes, John had a difficult time keeping the bike from slipping. When climbing, the front wheel often lifted right off the ground due to the weight of a Dani riding in the rear. When that happened, John pushed himself forward till he was hanging over the handlebars jockey style to bring the wheel down. "It's quite a sensation when on one side you have the steep mountain face, and on the other a drop-off into a seemingly bottomless chasm. The trail is too narrow to do anything but stay on the machine and somehow wrestle it to the ground," he told colleagues.

Well into his motorcycling experience, he found out that he should have been using a special oil mix with the gasoline, instead of regular oil. He discovered that this was why the spark plugs carboned over and the machine got very hot. As he drove up the steep mountain in second gear, suddenly the motor would quit. There on the mountainside he had to remove the spark plug from the sizzling motor, and put in a new plug. Fifteen minutes later the same thing happened. Sometimes he changed plugs seven times between Karubaga and Kanggime, often on steep ascents where it was hard to keep the cycle from sliding backwards. But the Lord gave him the ability to do what was required and protected him as well.

"John will take any risk to keep an appointment with the Danis," a co-worker commented. If John told the Danis he would be there at a certain time, they would be waiting for him. That was the case each Friday when John and his Dani passenger from the Bible school pulled into Kanggime. Usually a hundred or more pastors and elders were singing and waiting for their mentor. Bruno DeLeeuw, who ministered to the Danis during the week, was with them.

First there was a time for the Danis to ask questions on the lesson of the week before. Then John taught for ninety minutes from the Book of Romans, bringing in both doctrinal study and Christian ethics. One day John dealt with the biblical principle in Philippians 2:4 of looking after the interests of others. "Tekola, why should we as Christians look after the needs of someone else?"

"Because God wants us to."

"Why do you think God wants us to?"

"God loves the other person too, even though he may not be our clansman."

"That's right, but why can't God *himself* look after the other person's welfare—why should we become involved?"

He had to think that one through. Wuninip volunteered, "God's Spirit now lives in us, and we express *his* love by doing what pleases him."

On Fridays, after teaching the pastors and elders, John also met with the Kanggime Church Council. In periods when he supervised all of the Toli churches, he traveled to Mamit as well.

12 Bold Moves

Muta was often John's passenger on these motorcycle trips to Kanggime. Muta did not attend Bible school, but over the years he and Leleki had completed about 80 percent of the Bible school program in John's "household" class. Muta had excellent rapport with people, and he, along with several other Dani men, showed a special aptitude for business which John encouraged them to use. John had determined before God that the Danis would not be financially exploited as so many emerging people had been, especially those living in the interior. He felt that the Danis didn't need foreigners to run their commerce, that they should be able to control their own money flow. He believed that as a naturally aggressive people, they could learn to buy and sell as well as trade.

From the start, the Danis had wanted the things the missionaries had—knives, axes, salt, towels. And mirrors. In Daniland there was no such thing as still water where they could see their own reflection; so everyone wanted a mirror. The Danis often had asked the missionaries to buy such items for them at the coast. At first all payment was on the barter system, with trade goods exchanged for vegetables or a few hours of weeding in the Dekkers' garden. Then the Danis began sending the fine vegetables they were growing to the coast as a cash crop. Soon there was so much trade going on for the people of Kanggime that John set up a *toko* (store) with one of the older Dani men in charge.

"Let's set up a co-op store supervised by the church," John suggested. "The people can get a fair price, and any profits can go to the church." Since the Danis did not know how to add or subtract, he taught them to use small electronic calculators from Hong Kong. When he flew to the coast, he took several Danis along to show them how to buy from the stores—how to carefully dicker with the merchants to get a fair price. He was able to pass on his earlier experience in retailing. Soon Muta and others were chartering a plane on their own, flying out potatoes, cabbages, bananas, and other produce. With the money they received for these items at the coast, they paid cash for their purchases— a planeload of such sure-to-sell items as knives, axes, spades, salt, soap, matches, towels, blankets, flashlights, kerosene, canned milk, cookies, and their favorite wrapped hard candies. For men they bought shirts and running shoes, for the women skirts, T-shirts, blouses, and fine Indian beads. Dani women, having their own sense of fashion, wouldn't buy just anything. "Please bring clothes in black, white, and red"—their favorite colors. So the Dani Christians took control of the money flow. As they cornered the market, the church prospered by it.

Some community development ventures were not so successful. Thinking of the need for fresh milk for Dani children, and the high cost of powdered milk, John flew in a heifer and a bull calf. After a calf was born, John told the Danis to take it away from its mother and let it have only part of the milk. "Then we will have some for the Dani babies whose mothers are short of milk," he explained. A week later John returned to Kanggime to find the calf pen empty. "Where's the calf?"

"Oh, Tolibaga, it was bawling and we felt sorry for it, so we put it by its mother." Future attempts didn't fare much better. He tried to distribute a few calves around the district, but one fell over a cliff, two fell into toilet holes, and another just died. The bull had an accident and killed itself. The Danis decided to slaughter the remaining cow and have a village feast, since they had no refrigeration to keep the meat.

"Chickens are better, Tolibaga," the Danis told him. "We kill one and eat it all."

Goats seemed a good idea too, but they got goiters because of the iodine deficiency in the soil. Frank Clark at Mamit was exceptionally good at animal husbandry and developed a fine herd of purebred pigs for breeding stock. This was most important because pigs still rated tops with the Danis. Dave Martin at Karubaga brought in honey bees from Australia to the Toli area. This provided another good cash crop and was a food the Danis enjoyed.

The Kanggime church had been financially independent from the start, but what it felt called of God to do would require a great deal more financial backing. John was on the lookout for other food items that the Danis could sell for cash, as well as provide them with additional nutrition.

The Kanggime Church Council had decided that anyone going on a mission from the Dani church must have the full approval of the church. This applied to everyone—house help, carpenters, airstrip builders, or literacy workers. In its brief experience the church had learned that some had gone out who did not behave themselves and were a reproach to the name of Christ.

John approved of this policy, but sometimes it was troublesome for him, as when RBMU personnel who needed workers called and said, "John, can you get us some volunteers to work on the airstrip right away?" At the time the call came in, John might be talking to a Dani who was a hard worker. "Do you want to go?" John would ask him, and without checking with the church John would have this help on the plane headed for the project.

The elders came to John. "Why did you do that? There's a problem with this man—he owes money, and things aren't right between him and his wife. You should have checked with us." John apologized.

Another time a couple had volunteered to go, but the church was slow making a decision. "Haven't you given your approval yet?" John asked the elders.

"We'll talk about it."

"But the plane is coming—we have to get them out of here."

John put them on the plane, later telling the Dani leaders, "So much money is involved! We can't have a plane fly in for nothing!"

The Dani church leaders were gracious, but unbending. "Tolibaga, please do not do that again."

"Listen, I waited and waited for you to decide," John shot back, "and I checked on them with a couple of local people."

"Tolibaga, there *is* a problem. That is why we didn't get back to you. This man has been accused of an indiscretion with a girl. There is no proof, just questions. So we hesitated. If it's proven that there has been fornication, we will order him back. We just want to warn you."

"I'm so sorry; I've done it again."

The elders consoled, "It may be all right. We'll pray for that man. Tolibaga, we love you."

Bitbet was one of the first to go out from the Kanggime church as a trained missionary to the unreached. Dani Christians from the Toli Valley area had been involved in missionary efforts as early as 1960 when Danis from the Ilaga area had traveled with C & MA missionary Gordon Larson and shared their newfound faith. When the RBMU missionaries pioneering among the Yali found many villages open to the gospel, they challenged the Danis: "Are there any who will help us?"

Kanggime Christians volunteered and soon began going out in large numbers to assist various missionary efforts, working first as general helpers. While some went only for adventure, most went to take the gospel to the unreached. Between 1963 and 1965 graduates of the Kanggime literacy schools assisted Western missionaries in developing literacy programs in several areas.

In the village of Kawem on the south coast, Tim Wyanggurik had persevered as a literacy teacher for more than two years after graduating from John's literacy class. As Tim taught basic literacy to the Kayagars, he kept on learning and increasing his own language ability. He also became very aware of the great spiritual need in that coastal area and wrote to Bitbet, his former Kanggime classmate: "Now that you have graduated from Bible school, maybe you will consider coming to this area. The Kayagar language is very difficult, but you can learn it. Then you could take the gospel to the villages along the river.

"As for me, I have witnessed here, but to teach and to disciple believers I need training such as you have had. Soon I will be coming home to attend Maranatha Bible School."

Bitbet was eager to be such a pioneer. When he and Worop graduated from Bible school, they returned to their own village of Egoni in their Kanggime district to work under the supervision of the local church. All Bible school graduates were to serve a year in their home church before being sent out as missionaries. After only a few months in his home church, Bitbet spoke to his elders: "In Bible school and in our churches, Tolibaga continually has been telling us to share with others the truths God has blessed us with. Tolibaga has told us about the Kayagar people who live on the Cook River near the headwaters of the Kronkel on the south coast. Some of the Bible school students went there to help after their first year of school and found these people have hard hearts. Some are can-

nibals and head hunters. Since Tim has written about the great
need there, I have a desire to go and teach the people what
Tolibaga has been teaching us."

"Is your wife in agreement?" the Egoni pastor and elders asked.

"I don't know," Bitbet admitted. Although Bitbet obviously adored Worop, customarily in Dani culture there was little talk between husband and wife; she did her job, he did his.

"Bitbet, you shouldn't be asking about this if your wife
does not know what you want to do," the elders counseled.

When Bitbet talked to Worop, he discovered that she
too wanted to share the blessings of God with the needy tribespeople who lived near the big water.

The church didn't hesitate to approve Bitbet. Because
of his former work in the church, the elders waived the usual
one-year apprenticeship. Only six months after Bitbet's graduation from SAM in 1969, the church sent word to John: "Bitbet is ready."

John radioed, "Wonderful! John McCain is waiting for
him. Two weeks from this Friday, when the sun is up, the
plane will come to Kanggime to pick up Bitbet and his family."

In Bitbet's village, his relatives and friends made a feast
and brought presents: an extra net bag, soap, a towel or two,
and potatoes for the journey. Then, as part of the Sunday service, Bitbet and Worop were brought to the front where the
pastor and elders laid hands on them. The pastor prayed,
"Lord, you are the God of Heaven and earth. Your servants,
Bitbet and Worop, are going to the coast. You are going to be
there as much as you are here. You have made yourself known
to us through Tolibaga; now make yourself known to others
through Bitbet."

On the day before the plane was due, Bitbet and Worop
and their two children said their good-byes. Then, accompanied by friends who helped carry their *barang* (possessions),
they walked to Kanggime. One carried Bitbet's box of trea-

sured Bible school books on his shoulders; another balanced a box containing soap, Bitbet's bush knife, steel axe, lantern, towels, and salt. Their clothes were wrapped inside a sleeping mat made of pandanus leaves sewn together. The blankets were carried in one net bag, the cassava roots, cobs of corn, potatoes, and bananas in another. In Kanggime they stayed overnight with friends, to be ready for an early morning departure.

Before daybreak, Bitbet and his wife hurried to the river to bathe and to dress for the trip. Since they could not go to the Kayagar people in traditional Dani attire, friends had given them Western clothes. In Kawem where they would be learning the Kayagar language, the men wore shorts. Quickly they ate a cold potato. Then word came from John. "It's time to weigh in." They gathered up their *barang*.

"Bitbet, I want to go, but—" Worop hesitated.

"But what, Worop?"

"I'm afraid to go in the *wururu!*"

Fifty or more people were clustered at the strip when the six-seater, single-engine Cessna 185 circled and touched down on the 800-yard grass strip. While the pilot unloaded a drum of kerosene and packed Bitbet's gear in the pod (a cargo bay under the fuselage), the departing missionaries exchanged final embraces and popped knuckles in farewell to family and friends. When everyone had cleared the strip, John gave the thumbs up, all-clear sign. As the plane taxied down the strip, there were final waves. Then the little plane picked up speed, lifted skyward, and headed down the valley, zigzagging through the passes and over the ranges toward the south coast. Bitbet, who had flown once with John and Helen to the north coast, saw that Worop was looking very grim and clutching her baby tightly at every bump. Even though he had flown before, he wasn't exactly a veteran flyer himself.

After almost two hours in the air, they touched down on a grass strip located beside the black Eilanden River where a float plane was tied up at the dock. The pilot transferred their *barang* to the Cessna 180 and they taxied down the river, carefully avoiding the floating logs. Then, in a flurry of spray, they lifted up, just missing the treetops. In only fifteen minutes the float plane landed at Kawem, John and Glenna McCain's pioneer station deep in the sago swamps forty miles upriver from the coast.[1]

John McCain waited on the dock as the Dani missionaries haltingly stepped into a new world. Already the steamy jungle air enshrouded them. *Can sweet potatoes grow in this swamp?* Bitbet wondered. *What a strange language the people are speaking! And it is so hot.* The temperature was above 100° and dropped only to 70° at night.

We didn't need to bring our blankets. Worop wished she didn't have them to carry.

John and Glenna McCain greeted them warmly while the McCain children made friends with the Dani children. "We have a house ready for you." Bitbet and Worop smiled, but looked warily at the little house on poles.

13 Reaching Out

"Oh, Bitbet, will it always be this hot?" Worop sat up on the palm mat, then looked out the door of the tiny house on "legs," hoping to see even the slightest movement of air. Not a leaf or reed stirred.

Bitbet detected a slight tremble in her voice. "I hope not Worop, but Tim warned us that the nights would not be cool as they are in Kanggime."

"It's so muggy—and so still!" She breathed deeply, as though to cut through the heavy air and draw in a breeze, if there was one somewhere.

"We will get used to it after a while, Worop. God will help us live in this climate, just as he did Tim."

Worop didn't for a minute doubt God's ability to do anything, but at the moment she felt smothered. God knew that too, she was sure. She asked him to help her cope with the climate, to enable her to learn the language, to cook and eat the strange food, and to be friendly to the village women. Finally she slept.

Bitbet's mind was anything but still. New words, strange faces, dugout canoes, and thoughts of home chased each other like whirling propellor blades until sleep eventually took over.

The couple wakened to the same oppressive air. Although the rising sun assured them it would be even hotter during the day, Bitbet and Worop knew that they had to bear down and learn the difficult Kayagar language. As they tried to concentrate on the words of the new language, they wiped the ever-present moisture from their faces and hands. There were no primers or language-learning materials for them. They knew only the Dani language and a bit of Indonesian Bitbet had picked up at Bible school. Since the McCains didn't know Dani, the only language they had in common was Indonesian. Trying to learn the Kayagar language under these circumstances was difficult, but each day Bitbet and Worop faithfully met with their mentors. In their little house overlooking the water they practiced saying Kayagar words to one another. And each hot day Bitbet looked more longingly at the river.

One especially hot afternoon after language study, while Worop went to the house to care for the little girls, Bitbet stepped outside to watch small children bobbing in the river near the shore. *It must be shallow there—I'm going to join them and cool off a bit*. He jumped in and sank like a stone in the deep river. Instinctively beating the water with his arms, Bitbet surfaced long enough to get a little air before going under again. As he came up, he reached out for some grasses overhanging the bank.

"Help!" It was a weak cry, but a Kayagar woman walking nearby heard him. She grabbed his arm and dragged him out of the water. "Worop, come quickly," she yelled.

Who is calling me with such urgency? Worop wondered as she hurried from the house. There was Bitbet on the river bank gasping for breath.

"I pulled your husband from the river." Worop didn't know much of the language, but she caught the word "river" and could see that Bitbet was wet. Kneeling beside Bitbet, the Kayagar woman held his mouth open and poked a twig down his throat to make him throw up. As Worop saw what to do, she took the twig and gently continued the technique. Whether it was this or God's intervention is not clear, but Bitbet threw up the water and soon could breathe normally. He and Worop thanked their Heavenly Father.

With renewed respect for the perils of the river, they kept close watch on their children. Not long after Bitbet's experience their little girl, Mina, was playing near the edge of the water and fell in. Bitbet was nearby, but the steep bank prevented him from seeing her right away. *She was just there!* "Mina! Mina!" In alarm he ran to the steep bank and looked over. His beloved Mina was in the water! As she disappeared from sight, Bitbet jumped. The nonswimming Dani was again in the water. Two lives were at stake this time. Just as Bitbet managed to get a hold on Mina he felt strong arms pulling him out of the water. Saying *"Terima kasih!"* (the common Indonesian expression of appreciation), Bitbet quickly bent over little Mina who obviously had swallowed water.

"O Lord, help me know what to do—please save my little daughter!" As he called on God, he grabbed a twig and tickled the back of Mina's throat as the Kayagar woman and Worop had done for him. She too threw up the water. He carried the limp little girl to the house, where Worop joined him in thanking God for saving Mina and Bitbet.

Bitbet pondered the problem of the river in the life of his family. *Will we ever be able to swim? Maybe we should stay away from the river, but that won't be possible. I have to learn to paddle a dugout—how else can we go anywhere here?* These were problems for Danis wanting to take the gospel to villages downriver.

After several months of language study in Kawem, Bitbet and his family were invited to live in Ogotut, a village where there was no witness. Bitbet had visited there once and being a winsome man, he had made friends. Despite not being fluent in the language, he knew how to use what he had learned and made good contacts in the village. He accepted the invitation.

Again they had to face the reality of the river. Along with another Dani who had come to help them, they loaded their gear into the dugout and set out downriver. The tippy craft was more than the inexperienced Danis could handle and it capsized, spilling out the nonswimming occupants and their belongings.

"The children!" Cries went to God as well as to each other as they floundered, reaching out for their daughters with one hand and the overturned dugout with the other. "Hang on to the dugout, Worop—it won't sink!" The other Dani already had a tight hold on it too. The troublesome craft that had dumped them so unceremoniously into the water became their means of getting to shore. Pushing, guiding it in the direction of the bank, the tired Danis finally stood on land.

The extent of their loss hit them hard. Everything was gone—the ax, mosquito netting, soap, New Testament, and clothing. Disheartened, they did the only thing they could do. They returned to Kawem. Since there was only one way to do that, they got into the dugout—carefully. A nervous Worop held the little girls very still as the novice paddlers again tried to manage the tippy dugout.

Safely back in Kawem, Bitbet wrote Tolibaga about the loss. "God has given me all these things. He will replace them." Then he gave the letter to John McCain, who put it on the next MAF plane to Kanggime—not overnight air mail, but a welcome link with Tolibaga and the home church.

Once more they set out downriver to Ogotut, where the village people helped Bitbet build a house. To keep it out of the water, the house had to be built on pilings made from sturdy iron wood poles. Sheets of beaten palm bark formed a floor, woven reeds the walls, and palm thatch the roof. When the house was finished, Bitbet planted a sweet potato garden, but the water flooded it. Even if it hadn't, the soil was too sour to produce good potatoes, Bitbet reluctantly admitted. "We too will have to eat sago." Knowing she had to learn to prepare it,

Worop went with the women of the village to cut down the sago palm, scoop out the heart, and then wash, knead, and boil it into a gluey *papeda*. It was tedious but not as time-consuming as growing sweet potatoes. With lemon squeezed over it, their new staple food was quite delicious.

Bitbet sometimes went with the men to hunt wild boar, which were plentiful and good eating. Three-inch sago grubs fried crisply over a fire were another delicacy they learned to enjoy. And there was always fish. With this abundance of food, Worop was happy, because it was the Dani woman's job to feed the family.

Trying to avoid the diseases of the south coast was more difficult than accepting the new diet. One of the first Danis to the area had picked up a tropical disease and died very quickly. Bitbet and Worop were frequently exposed to cascado, a spreading fungus infection which could cover the entire body with flaking scales. They took care to wash themselves thoroughly, especially after sitting in Kayagar houses. Though Bitbet did not have medical training, he knew some common medical problems and what to do for them.

In a letter to Tolibaga, Bitbet reported another problem of adjustment: the men of Ogotut wore no clothes.

In the evenings Bitbet sat with them, teaching them the things of the Lord, while Worop taught the women, haltingly, using their meager Kayagar vocabulary. In spite of their limitations, the Holy Spirit blessed their efforts, and soon there was a group of believers.

At the Kanggime airstrip John was organizing items that had been brought by the Danis to go out on the next airplane. "What is this?" John asked in astonishment as he saw mounds of gourds and string skirts at the plane loading zone.

"Punuk wrote that the Sawi heathen men are going about without anything on, and asked that we send gourds," replied one of the village Danis who had brought the shipment. "We're sending the skirts to the Yali women who wear only little tufts of bark. Now that they are becoming God's children, they should be clothed decently."

John shrugged. *All these years I've been careful not to impose Western culture on them—not make them wear my kind of clothes. They sat in Bible school in string skirts and gourds. Now they are exporting their culture to the tribes they are evangelizing! I wonder how Bitbet is dealing with these problems.* John was able to keep the Danis from sending the gourds, explaining that they were too bulky and breakable to ship. Then he taught them that gourds would not be acceptable on the south coast since they did not grow gourds there. He also explained that the government was urging the men there to wear pants.

In addition to serving as advisor to all the Toli Valley churches, John also counseled Danis going out as missionaries to other areas. As he and a church leader talked about church matters one day, the Dani said, "I wonder how our missionaries are doing."

"Maybe we should visit them to find out," John suggested.

"A good idea! Will you do that?"

And so John planned a trip to the south coast to see Bitbet and Worop. In the little MAF plan he followed the same route the missionary couple had taken almost a year before, and he landed in the same sultry place.

"Tolibaga!" Bitbet was waiting to take him downriver to Ogotut. John hoped that Bitbet's ability with a dugout had improved. Soon the Dani was paddling them down the river as though he had been doing it all his life.

At Ogutut approximately seventy-five villagers, mostly believers, were gathered by the river. Bitbet spoke first, introducing John. "This is my father, who taught me all I have been teaching you. Now he will speak to you."

John said in Dani, *"Ayee! Norewi wa!"* And Bitbet
translated, "Greetings!" Dogs were fighting and yelping; children were running in and out of the crowd. John raised his
voice above the din. "I am so thankful you have responded to
the words of God as given to you by Bitbet."

Later, when John and Bitbet talked alone, the Dani
brought up some of the problems he had. "Oh, Tolibaga, we're
having a hard time teaching them Christian songs."

"But, Bitbet, those are Dani Christian songs. You are
singing God's words in your own language and in your own
music. Now you will have to help them put God's words to
their kind of music." Bitbet understood, remembering that
John had observed that rule with the Danis, and had not insisted that they sing Western songs.

Some time after John's visit, and just when the church
at Ogotut was growing nicely, the government decided that
the people of this village should move into a larger center.
Because he wanted to do pioneer work, Bitbet accepted an invitation from the village leaders in Amyam to come and teach
there.

Amyam had been known as a Catholic village. In some
parts of the island the Roman Catholic missions had exerted a
positive influence, but there were problems on the south coast.
In Amyam the Catholic schoolteacher's affairs with some of
the local women had so enraged the people they forcibly drove
him from their village. As the Kayagars in Amyam began to
put their trust in Jesus Christ and to be baptized, the priest
became incensed. "You're stealing my sheep," he accused Bitbet. "These people belong to the Catholic church. You're stealing them for your own purposes."

"Ask the people," Bitbet suggested. "Your teacher was
an adulterer who offended them many times. They asked me to
come and to teach them. Let's see who they choose now."

As Bitbet stood in one place, and the priest in another a
hundred yards away, they asked the people to line up behind

the one they wanted to teach them. When only three identified themselves with the priest, he was furious. "You should leave anyway; this is my territory!" he insisted.

Bitbet was just as insistent. "As soon as the people want me to leave I'll go; otherwise I'll stay and teach them from the Word of God." He stayed three years, until John McCain asked him to take over the work at Kawem while the McCains were on furlough. That year Bitbet went back and forth, preaching the gospel and shepherding the churches in both places.

During McCain's absence the Catholics, who were enraged that Amyam had become mostly Protestant, decided to move into a place called Amaro where McCain had been preaching. One of the Christians sent word to Bitbet that the Catholics had started to put up a church there. When Bitbet and two other believers arrived, they hacked through the vines with their bush knives to take apart the building. The villagers who did not want to follow the Lord took sticks and began to beat Bitbet and his companions. Finally both sides agreed, "Let's settle this before a government official."

Several canoe loads—the Catholic priest and teacher, Bitbet and an elder, and other village folks—paddled to the coast. After hearing both sides, the government official took a strong stand, telling the Catholic group, "This is an area where the gospel was being preached. You had no business going in to build another church." This was a real victory for the gospel and an encouragement to Bitbet and the Christians.

Farther downriver in Haipon, the people were also having problems with an immoral Catholic schoolteacher. Many times the police had to come in to straighten out the trouble he was creating. A Haipon man who had known Bitbet at Ogotut and Amyam said, "At Amyam there is a man of God, an honest, moral teacher who really preaches the Word of God. Let's run out of town this renegade who causes us so much trouble, and ask this teacher from Amyam to come here." They sent a delegation to Bitbet in Amyam, and he agreed to move to their village after Nggeri, another Dani missionary, arrived from Kanggime to take his place. They built a nice house for Bitbet and when it when was finished went upriver with many canoes to bring Bitbet and his family from Amyam. By then Nggeri had come from Kanggime and moved into a house Bitbet had built for him.

Going to Haipon meant learning another language, Atohwaim, Because of the government influence all along the river, there were some who could understand Indonesian, but their heart-languages were Kayagar or Atohwaim. While Bitbet learned Atohwaim, one of the men was able to interpret for him so that even during this time of learning the language many came to faith in Jesus Christ as a result of Bitbet's teaching.

Bitbet decided to introduce his old trade to Haipon, which was located in a timber area. In early 1962, when Bitbet was a witness man, John had sent him to Mamit to take a carpentry course. After he had learned how to build houses, and to operate a pit saw, Bitbet had set up a pit-sawing project in some of the Toli Valley villages. In Haipon he taught the men how to roll the heavy logs from the river up a ramp to the saw, and to slice through the hard wood quickly and neatly. With their newly acquired skill the Christians from Haipon were in demand as carpenters, especially by the government. As a result of being able to earn money, the Haipon church had more means to help others than did some of the village churches.

Seeing the growth of the Haipon church and the change in the life of the entire community because of it, the people of Kawem said regretfully, "We were the first to hear the gospel from missionaries, but we did not respond to it. Now these people, speaking a different language, are ahead of us." Through the witness of Haipon believers people from Kawem became Christians, were baptized, and followed the Lord. Bitbet's work touched lives all up and down the river.

Au, a man who came to the Lord under Bitbet's ministry, became a strong leader in the Haipon community. When Au had a burden for the lost in other areas, the church in

Haipon sent him downriver where he established churches in two places. Later he developed a traveling ministry to teach and build up churches as they sprang up in villages along the river.

Semit, another Haipon man, had been looked up to by his people as a fearless warrior who had killed many men, and as a leader of the village when he first heard the gospel. Semit was so deeply touched by the Word and by Bitbet as a person, he announced to the village that he was adopting Bitbet into his family. Semit called the people together, took a piece of cooked sago, rubbed it over Bitbet's skin, and then ate it. "Now Bitbet is flesh of my flesh. I have taken him as my son. From here on he will bear my name, Kagaromit."

Among the Haipon people, this adoption is a stronger bond than that of natural family. Soon the custom found its way into the Haipon Communion service. As the pastor takes a piece of sago and breaks it, he says: "This signifies our Lord's body which was broken for us. We eat, we partake of him. He is our life. Just as we adopt people into our family by rubbing sago over our skin and eat it up to signify that they become part of us, so Jesus Christ becomes part of us as we partake of the sago. Although it is only a sign, in a real way he has become a part of us and we are part of him. He is ours, and we are his forever."

One day Bitbet visited a man he had befriended in another village. As Bitbet entered the house, he saw the man's wife obviously ill and lying on the floor. "What's wrong with your wife?" Bitbet asked.

"She has been sick for a long time. A barb from the fin of a poisonous fish penetrated the skin next to her knee. It is still in there." Bitbet saw that the leg was very swollen, and the woman was in intense pain. "What is that you have under your knee?" he asked.

"A Bible," they replied. "A visiting leader from the

Catholic church told us if we put the Bible there, the sickness will go away."

Bitbet saw that they were using the Bible as a fetish, mixing Christian beliefs with the old animistic religion. "It is true that the Bible contains God's Word," Bitbet said. "It tells us about the Creator God and what he has done. It tells us about Jesus Christ and how we can know him, but the Book cannot heal you. Only God can. Do you want me to pray to God for you?"

"Yes, yes, please pray."

So Bitbet took the Bible away and put it on the floor beside him. While the others were crossing themselves, Bitbet prayed very simply: "O Lord, we know that all power belongs to you. You alone have the power of healing. Will you please intervene in this sickness and heal this woman. We know you can do it. We commit her to you."

That night Bitbet was wakened by the woman's excited husband. "Bitbet! You prayed for my wife and she is healed! You've got to come and see what has happened. The place where the barb was hiding has opened up, and the barb has come out. She is well again! I couldn't wait until morning to tell you!"

Bitbet hurried to the house where he found the woman sitting up. Her leg was its normal size, and she could bend her knee. The pain was gone. As the people rejoiced, the husband wanted to give Bitbet some large crocodile skins. "No, no," Bitbet protested. "I cannot take pay. I didn't do anything. God has done this for you that you might believe."

Still they insisted that Bitbet must take something. "I would like to have something from you, but you must let me pay the regular price because it was not my power but God's that healed your wife. I cannot take pay for what God has done."

Bitbet urged the man to place his faith in the living Christ rather than in a printed book. "God has shown himself mighty on your behalf so that you will turn from your superstitions and believe."

"Bitbet, we'll build a church if you will come and live among us and teach us," they pleaded, but for the time Bitbet had to leave.

When Bitbet's daughter Tabita completed her sixth grade, she and others her age were required to go for an examination to a government school on the coast. Their teachers asked Bitbet if he would accompany them. "We have heard that some of the teachers at that school are immoral, and we don't want our girls going there unless our missionary accompanies them." So Bitbet set out with the teachers and students in dugout canoes to a place downriver, where they were to be picked up by a larger boat and taken on to the examination point.

As they were about to board the larger boat, which was operated by the Catholics, the priest recognized Bitbet. "You're not coming on my boat. You have supplanted us and driven us out of three villages. You have had our teachers thrown out and have built your churches. I'm not going to give you a ride anywhere." So Bitbet was left standing on the shore.

"Then we are not going either. We will stay with our missionary and the girls." The teachers marched off the boat and, with Bitbet and the students, set out on the trek overland.

After the examinations the local teacher arranged for them to be taken by a large seagoing canoe back to the mouth of the river where they had left their dugouts. When a wind came up, a very high wave washed over the canoe, filling it with water and sending it under.

"Father! Father!" Tabita called as she was swept from his sight by the waves. Bitbet had still not learned to swim, but his *kaleng* bobbed up beside him like a lifesaver. Bitbet recognized it for what it was and grabbed the handle of the large watertight container holding his belongings. As waves washed over him, Bitbet hung on, remembering past experiences with the river, and again called on God. "Lord, if you have no more work for me, I'm ready to come to you. But if you have further work for me to do, then you must save me from this." As he surrendered himself, he felt that the Lord was pushing him with the waves toward shore. Suddenly he felt the soft mud of the sea bottom under his feet. Standing there while waves crashed against the mangrove trees, he looked around for the others and again prayed. "O God, please lead me to my daughter." He knew she and the others could swim and felt they had made it to the shore. It took another ten minutes for Bitbet to wade through the knee-deep mud to the shore, where he began searching for the others.

He called, "Tabita! Tabita!" again and again. At last there was an answer. "Father!" Tabita and the others were together. "We were so afraid because you cannot swim—"

"God placed my *kaleng* right beside me," Bitbet told them.

"We have lost everything, but we were able to swim to shore."

Praising the Lord and strengthened in their faith, they returned to Haipon in the teacher's dugout.

One day in early 1983, while Bitbet was going about his work in Haipon, he had a visitor, an Indonesian Christian from another denomination. "Bitbet, we have heard how the people respond to your presentation of the gospel. Who is looking after you? How much do you get for a salary?" the visitor asked. Bitbet told him that he got only five dollars or so a month.

"If you join our denomination, we'll give you a good salary and more help. We'll build a bigger church and give you and your people all that you need." He had brought clothing and presents and stayed a couple of days trying to persuade Bitbet. But Bitbet was firm. "No, this is God's work. The Lord has led us through the Evangelical Church of Irian Jaya to start this work, and it is under its supervision that we do this. I do not feel that I should place this work, which the Lord has blessed, under a different denomination. Any time you want to come and preach here, it's all right with us, but we will not build another church. The Lord has given us a good work under the Evangelical Church. We will stay with it."

Bitbet was one of the dozens of Danis who with their wives and children went as missionaries to other areas of the island. The young churches applied what John had taught from the beginning: when God blesses you with something, give it to others. They understood that stewardship was giving of themselves and the message that had changed them.

Soon after the first Danis became Christians, several went to Ninia to the eastern highlands to work on the airstrip being built there. When the first Danis graduated from the literacy class, some of them went as literacy teachers among the Yalis at Ninia. Eventually twenty couples were in that area. A second outreach, at about the same time, was to the Kayagars of the south coast where Danis worked with Don Richardson among the Sawis and with John McCain among the Kayagars. Fourteen couples responded to those calls. In the mid- and late-sixties, thirty couples joined Costas Macris who had gone to pioneer the Lakes Plain district. Then, following the martyrdom of Stan Dale and Phil Masters in 1968, there was another push beyond Ninia to the more remote eastern highlands.

By the early 1970s the seventy-nine indigenous churches of the Toli Valley, with 13,000 baptized members, had sent out and were supporting more than sixty-five qualified missionary couples. This great missionary movement saw a beautiful blending of national and Western missionary skills. The Danis were more quickly accepted by the other tribes and could live right among the people in a way Westerners could not. On the other hand, the Western missionary brought expertise in language analysis, translation, medicine, airplanes, supplies, and a better understanding of doctrinal issues. As co-workers they complemented each other in a remarkable way.

No single Dani women were sent out as missionaries. It was not workable in the "man's world" cultures of the tribes. Some of the women engaged in ministries to women and girls, but most of their time was spent on the gardens and taking care of the home and children in an area where it is hard work just to get what is needed to live.

To finance this great missionary program, RBMU helped with travel expenses. But the Dani churches paid half of the airfares, as well as the living expenses of their missionaries.

For the Kanggime church, as for the whole Toli area, giving was a great joy—a time of celebration and feasting. These people spent far more of their meager income on their missionaries than on the home base. Once or twice a year as many as 2,000 people from five or six churches came together for an "offering day," bringing their offerings and food for the feast. First they dug the pits and got the *mbingga* and other food cooking. Then they crowded around examining the goods brought by each church for auctioning. No one officially served as master of ceremonies, but Pastor Wuninip picked up a rabbit and asked, "Who'll give 1,000 rupiahs?"[1]

"I'll give 700."

"Sold."

Then he held up a brown hen with legs tied and wings flapping. "Who'll give 1,500 rupiahs for this fine laying hen?" Wuninip raised his voice above the hen's noisy squawking.

At another pile, Pastor Wewonggen displayed a red *tawi*, a pandanus fruit nearly two feet long. "What will you offer for this big *tawi*? Do I hear 200 rupiahs? It's yours." A piglet went for 4,000 rupiahs, a string bag nicely worked with crocheted orchid fibers for 1,000 rupiahs. For months the people had raised animals and produce or crafted items to bring. For most, it was sacrificial giving.

John had helped the Kanggime Danis to become more self-sufficient economically through marketing vegetables, chickens, rabbits, and pigs, and by setting up co-op stores and

providing air transport. As he observed the mighty moving of
the Spirit, John realized that the Dani church needed more
cash to send and support missionaries and to help meet the
many needs on the field. John discussed this with Wuninip,
who understood. He was aware that Karubaga had developed
excellent vegetable gardens for cash market sale, providing
money for that district's churches. Kanggime needed a strong
cash crop that not only would bring in money for missions but
also provide additional protein. Protein deficiency and malnu-
trition among the children was an ongoing problem that concerned John.

John had read that peanuts were easy to grow and that
they were nutritious. Since he also loved to eat them, it was not
hard to decide to import peanuts.

First he decided to try out some roasted peanuts on his
witness class.

"I have a surprise for you—something for you to taste."
As he passed the peanuts from student to student, sounds of
"*abu meya*" and "*obeelom!*" were heard as one Dani after another expressed delight.

Then he went to see Wuninip. "Have some peanuts,
Wuninip."

"This is good, Tolibaga!"

"How would it be if I get some seed peanuts at the coast
and give some to the Kanggime church people to plant? Maybe
we will have the cash crop we are looking for to bring in more
money for missions."

Munching some more peanuts, Wuninip enthusiastically agreed. "I'll tell the people about it."

Soon peanuts were growing in all of the Dani gardens in
Kanggime. When the nitrogen-rich plants were dug back into
the soil, they improved the gardens. After a couple of years
each family had a peanut patch.

Since there was not a regular direct plane from Kanggime to the coast, only produce which would keep for some
time could become a commercial product. Since peanuts were

that kind of product, they soon became the big trade item. In preparation for shipping them to the coast, peanuts are dried on mats in the sun. Then they are packed in large gourds or string bags lined with pandanus leaves or tied in old shirts or plastic bags.

At one point the Danis found they had too many peanuts. "Why not make peanut oil?" it was suggested. "The pulp would make good feed for the pigs and chickens too." John ordered a machine, containers, and a sealing device. They were in business, but not quite. On the trial run, the peanuts were too moist. Then they couldn't find a person to oversee the project. When it didn't work as expected, they gave the equipment to a Bible and vocational training school at the coast for use in their coconut oil project.

Income from peanuts has financed much of the Kanggime church's missionary outreach. Everyone agrees that without peanuts, the missionary effort would be hopelessly strapped.

14 Hard Places

When Stan Dale returned to Australia for furlough in 1965, Costas Macris replaced him at Ninia for the year. As Costas quickly developed Yali primers, children and adults began to crowd into his literacy classes. He sent word to Kanggime: "Are there any Danis who can come over and help us?"

"We don't have trained evangelists, but we have literacy workers who can share the gospel with the Yalis as they teach."

And so seventeen Dani teachers went to Ninia, paid with funds that Costas raised. Even before they learned the Yali language, the teacher-evangelists fanned out through the mountains, preaching the gospel at every opportunity, using Dani Scripture portions and translating into Yali as they went —repeating and repeating. New Yali believers teamed up with them.

Even though it was a highland area with similar food, the Danis found it a hard place to live and work. It was a much higher altitude, about 6,600 feet, and on the rocky 45°–60° slopes with so much erosion and leaching of the soil, garden space was at a premium. The Yalis were reluctant to share plots that had been in families for years, even in exchange for bush knives and axes. Only occasionally would they rent or sell a small piece.

The Danis found that due to the poor soil, the potatoes were smaller and took longer to grow. The pigs were smaller, and even the people. The mountains, however, were steeper, and the nights were much colder above the clouds. More of the day was wrapped in mist.

In some villages the Dani evangelists were appalled to see the ground around the huts filthy with excrement, and the decomposing bodies of the dead placed on platforms in the trees to rot and smell. In many areas the people were cannibals, simply because human flesh tasted so good. An older Yali confided he had recently paid two men a pig to shoot and bring him the body of a young person from an enemy tribe. "It was so much softer than the flesh of pigs." The sensual old Yali smacked his lips with relish.

"That is wrong!" the Dani evangelist chastised him sternly. "You should not do that to someone who is made in the image of God. You can eat pigs, but you should not eat people. Even though you have done this bad thing, God still loves you and wants you to be his child and to become like he is," he told the old cannibal.

"Aren't you afraid that one day you'll end up in their stomachs?" John asked when the Dani recounted this to him during a visit there.

"No, the Lord is protecting us. We are here in his name. We don't need to be afraid." Fearlessly the Danis pushed deeper and deeper into the unknown, unreached areas of the eastern highlands and into the lowlands to the south.

As among Western missionaries, there were casualties. Nop was the sixth child born to his mother, but the first one to live. His father had been a prime warrior in his clan, and involved in witchcraft. In 1963 Nop and his wife moved to Kanggime so that they could hear God's Word. Eagerly they joined a young marrieds group and attended literacy classes each

morning. In the evening John further grounded them in the
Word. After attending Maranatha Bible School they responded to the call for help in the Lakes Plain area. But Nop
had a hard time identifying with the hostile people. Before
long he returned home to the Toli area where he pastored in
the home church for four years. Again he felt called of God to
reach out to those who had not heard the gospel. In 1973 when
the Netherlands Reformed Congregation (NRC) requested
help in the Langda area, Nop volunteered to go. When he arrived, NRC missionary Jan Louwerse asked him if he would
consider contacting the Ladji, traditional enemies of the
Langda people. He agreed to go.

Twice these dangerous warriors rebuffed him, but during his third attempt there was an earthquake accompanied by
a loud clap of thunder. Nop shouted to the people, "Can't you
understand—God wants to get through to you. He loves you
and wants you to listen to him."

"*Ayee*, this must be so. We must listen," the frightened
villagers agreed. All except Yonan, the chief, a man about
fifty. While the others listened to the Word of God in morning
and evening devotions and attended literacy classes, Yonan not
only refused to join in, but opposed the efforts. Nop had given
him several axes and knives, not to win him over to the gospel,
but to acknowledge him as chief. Yonan accepted these items
and indebted himself to Nop; yet he refused to honor the debt.

At times he spoke well of Nop; at other times he spoke
evil. He sat among the people who wanted to hear God's Word
and continually interrupted: "That's not so. Nop doesn't know
what he's talking about." After this heckling went on for some
time, an exasperated Nop gave the chief a kick in the rear and a
smack on the head with his hand. "We can't go on like this,
Yonan. If you kill me, you kill me," he said. When Yonan continued to disrupt meetings on three different occasions, Nop responded physically.

"You had it coming to you," the others told the chief.
"You shouldn't be speaking about Nop out of both sides of your

mouth. You should not oppose him for bringing us the Word of God." Only then did the chief settle down and come regularly to the services.

Laik, another graduate of the Bible school, went to work in an adjacent village where the people were known as even more fierce warriors. Laik took thirteen men with him to help build his house. As the group approached the village, they looked up and saw a line of fully armed warriors waiting for them on the crest of the hill. They looked every bit as ruthless as they had been depicted. "Laik, you go ahead and find out if they will accept us," his helpers suggested. Their reluctance was not lost on Laik, but instead of urging them to accompany him, he called on God to deal with the men on the ridge. "Lord, I can go alone, knowing that you can give them a fear in their hearts that will restrain them from killing me. But if I get killed, it's only my body."

He walked up to the warriors bristling with bows and arrows. The chief stepped forward, offering tobacco and a piece of potato as a sign to the other warriors that Laik and his party were not to be killed. The chief not only gave permission for Laik to build a house and live among them, but the people helped him build a church and learn the language.

Before going out as a missionary Laik had received instruction in basic medicines such as penicillin. As he gave out medicine, he prayed for the sick and saw some dramatic recoveries which made a strong impression on the people.

Although there were a great many candidates for baptism, Nop and Laik were careful to baptize only those who really understood the Word. These became elders in the church and went out teaching every weekend in different parts of the valley. Four of these converts went to Karubaga to attend Maranatha Bible School. Others of these who had come out of darkness became burdened for those who still had not heard the gospel. Led by Laik and Nop, in 1979 a group set out on a seven-day trek through two mountain passes to the south lowlands where they traded axes, mirrors, and salt with hunting and fishing parties. Over a three-year-period they made the long trip six times, exploring and opening the area for more frequent visits by evangelizing parties. As these groups probed farther, they found more unreached people and new languages requiring interpreters. As they went from village to village, staying in a different treehouse each night, people told them, "We have waited for the Word of God for a long, long time. We want to have an evangelist come stay with us." The Langda Christians were eager to do this, but Jan Louwerse, the NRC missionary, suggested, "Hold off until more experienced Danis can come to work with them. We have the helipad, but no real backup for medical needs." In the meantime the Langda Christians faithfully shared their newfound faith during frequent treks to the lowlands.

Wabinan was assistant paster of his home church near Kanggime when a call came from RBMU missionary Costas Macris in the Lakes Plain district. "We need help to open up this area. Who will come?"

"We will," Wabinan and his wife volunteered. Wabinan—exuberant, outgoing, fun, and loved by the young people—had participated in John's youth program and had walked two miles each morning to attend literacy classes. In the afternoons he was always eager to help John with work around the station. At sixteen Wabinan had completed the reading and writing program and returned to his own village to set up a literacy school. When the Bible school opened, he became one of the first students. His wife had a sunny disposition and was always helpful.

With the commendation of their home church, Wabinan, his wife, and young children flew north to the vast, low-lying basin between the interior and coastal mountain ranges. This area was the latest RBMU outreach and was a difficult one. Poisonous snakes and crocodiles lived in the sago swamps. From the same watery ground dense swarms of mosquitoes carried malaria to most of the human inhabitants. Situated almost on the equator at close to sea level, the climate was extremely hot and humid. And there were floods.

The MAF plane bringing Wabinan and Tigina landed on the airstrip which Costas and the Dani workers had managed to carve out of this wet jungle, on the only piece of land that wasn't under water more than once or twice a year. The house they were shown to was hardly more than a shack on stilts. The palm bark floor was rotting, and the mosquitoes found easy entrance through cracks in the reed walls and the open windows. After living there awhile, the usually optimistic Tigina was discouraged.

"Wabinan, I cannot have my baby here!"

"God will provide all we need; we must work and be patient," her husband reassured the tearful Dani woman.

Since they arrived at a time when there was no flooding, Wabinan set to work making a sweet potato garden. "Dumb Danis," local natives chided. "You can't make gardens here. Soon the floodwaters will come and cover the land, and we will be paddling our canoes over your sweet potatoes!"

Wabinan went ahead, carefully tending his garden to which he added pineapples, papayas, and banana trees. That first year no high-water covered his fine crop. "See, this is the way we Danis do it. This is the way God blesses. We have plenty and enough to share with you."

"One of these days the floods will come," the Kai people scoffed. And the next year the floods did come. Wabinan lost all his potatoes, but not the fruit. The following year the high-water wiped out everything. A letter to John expressed his dismay. "What am I to do? I've been telling these people how God blesses, I have been sharing my potatoes with them, but now I have nothing."

There was no alternative but to accept sago as their staple food, along with wild pig and fish, which they shot with bows and arrows from their canoes. Although Wabinan nearly drowned learning, soon he could pole the dugouts skillfully through the swamps, shooting fish with a bow and arrow. They also discovered that the sago grubs were larger and juicier than the grubs of Kanggime. "But we get so hungry for the feasts of sweet potatoes of the highlands," they wrote home.

Many other adjustments and hardships faced the young missionary evangelist and his family. They had to constantly guard against the cascado fungus disease. The local people sat on Wabinan's floor and soon his family had it too, despite scrubbing all over with soap twice a day. And even though they took antimalarial medicine which the Macrises and John had supplied, they contracted malaria, though not as severely.

It was hard going financially, with only 3,000 rupiahs ($5) from the Dani church each month. They couldn't understand when Costas sent in a Christian Indonesian who had been trained as a schoolteacher and paid him more than Wabinan, though he had no family. He was provided a house with a zinc roof, to which he was accustomed, and nice furnishings. The mission did not want the Dani missionaries to become involved in local commercial enterprises such as crocodile hunting, for fear the ministry would suffer. Wabinan was able to earn a little extra by keeping the grass cut at the airstrip, but the 2,000 rupiahs he received each month for that chore covered only the cooking oil and three bars of soap.

The new missionaries found the Kai language very difficult to learn; yet a year after Wabinan's arrival, when John came to visit, a group was meeting in a schoolhouse and several believers had been baptized. Wabinan, always a favorite with youth, taught hymns and Scripture lessons to the children at school. When John returned to Kanggime, he raised money to build a house with an aluminum roof and screening on the windows for Wabinan and his family.

One day a missionary wife was bitten by a poisonous snake. "She's going to die," all the people wailed. The young missionaries prayed: "You have said in your Word that we will step on snakes and not die. We are here to represent you and your Word is true." The woman suffered only a slight toxic effect from poison.

The Dani missionary force in the Lakes Plain grew to more than twenty couples. Although great distances separated the missionaries, Costas and Alky Macris did an outstanding job of coordinating and backing the Dani evangelists. The Danis all loved Costas, whom they got to know when he worked with them on the Kanggime building projects and in literacy programs and in medical work during the Dekkers' furlough. The Danis knew they could depend on Costas to do what was best for them.

"Costas, our baby is very sick. Can you get a plane right away," they would call in on the radio. They knew Costas would do all possible to get a sick child to the hospital. He strongly felt that the mission should look after the Dani missionaries as it did the Westerners.

"We must have at least one aircraft based in the Lakes Plain district," Costas insisted at mission council meetings. "We have had Dani missionary children die because they were in a remote area and the MAF plane did not get to them in time, or someone decided that the Danis were overanxious and did not really need to be flown out."

Costas believed in letting the Danis take over as soon and as totally as possible. To aid them, he and Alky provided a support ministry. Once or twice a year the twenty couples involved in evangelism—a total of fifty or sixty including their families—met with the eighty Dani Christian workers from the airstrips, schools, and the sawmill. On one such occasion Costas arranged for the Dekkers to come in for a week's teaching and encouragement.

The men had many long talks about problems on the field. "Toli, these people do some horrible things," one of the missionaries confided to John one day. "They eat the testes of dead people, and they mix the juices of the dead with their sago. But then we did some bad things ourselves before we became God's children."

Helen had separate teaching and counseling times with the women, listening to their tragedies and triumphs.

Ngget was another Dani missionary who had taken his family to live in a remote area of the Lakes Plain where the people were primitive and cannibalistic. Ngget had been visiting these people for some time when they invited him to come and live among them. He learned their language and taught them about the Lord. Toward the end of the year he told them that other people on the island were planning to have a big feast to celebrate God sending his son into the world. "Can we have a feast here also?" the people asked. After it was agreed they could, they all went to the jungle to cut sago palms. A tree fell on an important man of the village, injuring him severely. They carried him to the airstrip while Ngget got on the radio to RBMU personnel: "We have a desperately injured man who must be taken to hospital immediately."

The mission plane picked up the man, along with a friend to accompany him to the closest government hospital at Womena, but the man died soon after arrival at the hospital. Since it was against the MAF policy to transport bodies, there was no way to get the dead man home. The MAF plane returned to the man's village to pick up some of his friends and flew them to Womena to witness the cremation, and then returned his friends to their village. This upset the people. As they grumbled someone asked, "Who suggested this feast in the first place?"

"Ngget. He's to blame for the death." As the crowd hysteria grew, someone yelled, "Let's get him and kill him!"

Ngget overheard this. Quickly he grabbed his wife and children and fled into the jungle where, instead of an angry mob, they had to contend with high-water, thorns, and snakes.

After hiding out for four days, Ngget sneaked back to his radio and called the pilot: "Get us out of here; they want to kill me."

Another couple who chose to go to a hard place were Awut and Aretina. They were sent by the Kanggime church to Hum, a remote village in the eastern highlands. "You should not go there. They will kill you," Christians in Nipsan, a day's walk away, told them.

"We have been called by the Lord to go to these people to share the gospel so that they too can become God's children. If that means death, we are ready for it."

The MAF helicopter deposited them in the mountain-top village where on an advance trip Awut had built a little hut in the forest, apart from the village. During the first month there no one except the chief and his household came to visit them. Awut shared God's Word with them. "It will just take time until the others accept us," they thought as they moved ahead to learn the language. They stretched the rice they brought with edible leaves and roots which Awut found in the forest. "You should take your bush knife or axe with you," his wife urged when he went out alone.

"If the people attack me, I will not fight back. My life is in God's hands, for better or worse."

During this time the younger brother of the chief died from an arrow wound. When two evangelists from another area passed the site where the funeral was taking place, they saw people sharpening their axes. "Why are you doing this?" they asked. "We are going to kill those two Dani teachers who have come into our midst."

The Danis did not know that two years earlier a man from the village of Hum had contracted a disease in his leg and had been flown out to hospital where his leg had to be amputated. When the man returned to his village, the people were horrified, concluding his leg had been cut off and eaten. They vowed they would get revenge. Somehow the death of the chief's brother aroused the old feelings. They decided that these strangers who had recently come must share in the blame.

When the two evangelists saw the murderous intent of the Hum people, they hurried to the huts of Awut and Negitebat, another Dani who had come to the area. "You must leave at once." The missionaries fled to the forest, huddling there throughout the night without protection from the cold rain. At daybreak they went to Tapla, where another Dani missionary lived.

The next day the "friendly" chief found them there. "I went looking for you in your houses—why did you leave without telling me? Come, let us return."

Aretina was reluctant, but Awut said, "We have come to help these people. Since the chief is showing goodwill, we should do as he asks." So they went back to Hum with him. Negitebat pretended to the chief that he felt ill and remained with his family in Tapla.

Two days later, just at dusk, fourteen young boys from the Hum area came to visit Awut and Aretina. They sat around for awhile, appearing to be friendly. The young missionaries were ill at ease, yet were happy for the contacts.

When the boys returned and asked Awut to go with them to their garden to dig potatoes, Awut was suspicious because it was raining. Later that day, after the rain, he and Aretina went to their garden to make a fence. Awut didn't notice a wasp nest in the tree he was cutting down. As wasps swarmed and attacked Awut, he ran whooping from the garden toward the river. "He'll bathe in the water to cool the stings," Aretina thought.

When Awut didn't return right away, she decided he had gone to get leaves from the forest for their supper. She returned home and put the water on the fire to boil. As she waited outside the little house, she heard a distinct shout from Awut. Still he did not return. Darkness came. By this time Are-

tina was worried. She walked in all directions, calling, "Awut!
Awut!"

"What is wrong?" It was the chief.

"Awut has not come home!"

When the fourteen boys came along, the chief sternly
demanded, "What have you done? Aretina says her husband is
missing."

The chief went off with the boys and in a short time
came back carrying a stick with a little blood on it, and some
torn clothes which Aretina recognized as Awut's. "He fell out
of a tree and hurt his lower leg," the chief told her. "He'll be
back tomorrow." The chief then sent the boys to the next village to tell the missionaries there that Awut had hurt himself.
Then they left Aretina alone with her child.

"I don't believe them," Aretina thought. "They have
killed my Awut." As she settled her child for the night she tried
to resist the thought that Awut was dead. Her unborn child
stirred. Before daybreak, as soon as the birds began to sing, she
put her little girl on her shoulder and hurried along the rough
path in the semidarkness.

And there she found him where they said Awut had
been hurt, lying partially inside a little hut, face up. Still
hoping he was alive she asked, "Why are you sleeping here?"
Then, kneeling beside him, she knew he was dead. His head
was twisted to the side and his neck had been broken. Blood
had come from his nose and ears, and bruises covered his body.
How did they kill him? she wondered. Then she had to deal
with the fact that Awut was gone.

Two hours elapsed before some of the men of Hum
came by, feigning surprise. Aretina asked them to carry Awut's
body to her home.

When they left, she tenderly arranged the body on a
sleeping platform and prayed. "We came here for the people,
sent by you, Lord. We knew we might get killed. Still it is very
hard." In her sorrow the Lord was near. For three days she did

not light a fire in the hut for fear Awut's body would decompose too fast. She cooked outside. Most of the time, she sat beside Awut's body, holding his hand, touching his cold brow. her little girl cried, knowing something had happened to her father, yet not understanding. For three days and nights Aretina kept watch, hoping someone would come. Finally on the fourth morning evangelists from another village arrived. They had not believed the story the boys had told them and thought they had better come to check. They prepared a funeral pyre, wrapped the badly decomposed body in a blanket, and placed it on the wood. After burying the few bones which did not burn, they planted sunflower seeds on the grave.

When their chore was accomplished, the saddened group walked to the next village where they radioed for a helicopter. Aretina flew home to her family. Two months later Awut's son was born. "God has been very near, and I have peace," Aretina said. "When God called us, we had to go. Live or die, we had to go."

15 Rebellion and
   Revival

Difficult problems had also faced the home churches and the
evangelical missions based on the island. The Indonesian government ruled out obtaining medicine from any country but
Indonesia. This created immense problems for the missions
which had been receiving free medicines from America and
Europe. Since the government could not immediately meet the
demands, tremendous shortages developed, especially of sulfa
drugs which were not available for almost a year. Even play
balls, an indispensable item in youth programs, became more
expensive.

　　The churches needed more and more training in order
to meet government requirements. The Dani Church, with the
help of RBMU personnel, added a junior high school to train
future Christian leaders and taught all classes in Indonesian.
Several Dani leaders went to the coast to take three years of
Bible training in Indonesian so as to be more competent in the
national language. In addition, more people needed training
in administrative skills and typing in order to prepare proper
reports for the government.

　　Still, in the two decades of missions to the Danis, many
national Christians reached full stature as responsible leaders

in the community and the church—a church burdened to reach the unevangelized. John believes this could not have been achieved without the unique teamwork among the nine evangelical missions comprising "The Mission Fellowship" (TMF): RBMU International, the Christian & Missionary Alliance, The Evangelical Alliance Mission, the Unevangelized Fields Mission, the Australian Baptist Missionary Society, the Asia Pacific Christian Mission, as well as the Netherlands Reformed Congregation (NRC) and the Zending Gereformeerd Kerken (ZGK-Holland) which held associate memberships, and the Missionary Aviation Fellowship, which provided air service for all of the others.

The TMF had 180 Western couples and single missionaries working on forty mission stations scattered throughout the interior and coastal regions. Each mission concentrated its efforts in a given area, avoiding competition or overlapping, and cooperated in opening new areas in Bible translation.

The C & MA operated an excellent school for the missionaries' children and handled piles of paperwork and government liaison on behalf of all TMF missionaries. At Regions Press RBMU took care of all the printing needs, producing New Testaments and literacy materials in dozens of languages. The missions joined hands in developing a Bible vocational school and shared personnel as needs arose—a school nurse, a bookkeeper, a cook for the annual conference. From the start the groups came together in a bond of love and oneness that made great progress together.

Remarkably, all this was achieved throughout a period of political unrest. Almost from the moment the mission teams arrived in Netherlands New Guinea, they wondered when they might be forced to leave. The island had been in Dutch hands until 1962, then under the United Nations until May 1963 when the Western portion of the island was turned over to Indonesia and became Irian Jaya. The eastern half which was under Australian mandate achieved independence in 1975 as Papua New Guinea.

From time to time since 1963, a rebel organization had tried to overthrow the Indonesian government. In 1976 this rebel movement surfaced again, attracting some of the young people—even children of church leaders. The youth went back to long, matted hair and to painting their faces and bodies for war. They started to make bows and arrows and spears. "We're going back to the old ways," they announced.

"How could you possibly want to go back to fear of spirits and the miseries of no food, of pain and cold, and war and death?" their parents asked them.

Most who joined the rebel forces were nominal Christians, young people who had come up in the church and perhaps were even baptized, but had not been born again. They thought the rebel movement offered excitement. Under the direction of leaders from Baliem Valley, the rebels drilled for hours and plotted to overthrow the government.

John tried to stay out of it. Most of the missionaries had determined that they would remain neutral, but increasingly the church leaders came to John with the same question. "Tolibaga, what shall we do? They are saying that it is a good thing to overthrow the government, that we will get the good jobs the Indonesians now have. They say that the Dutch will come back. We liked it better under the Dutch."

John decided that if he was going to take a stand, he needed to know more about the issues. When he heard there was to be a meeting of the rebels he wondered if he should attend. "John, it's too dangerous," Helen tried to dissuade him. But John asked his fellow-missionaries and the local government administrator, Rumbiak, whether they thought the trip was wise. They encouraged him to go.

John set off on his motorbike over the mountain and hiked the last half hour. He could hear whooping and hollering as he approached. When he arrived at a large clearing, John recognized many Christians mixed in with warriors from Baliem. Approximately 2,000 shouted, "We'll kill them!" as they waved their spears and snapped their bowstrings. John sat on the sidelines watching them go through their drill. Two whistles and they all dropped to their knees, two more whistles and they were up again and charging. He knew most of the Danis from the Toli area and when he found out who the leader was, he approached him and asked to speak.

"Our father wants to talk to us," the rebel chief announced. Everybody sat down.

John stood before them. "I can see you are enjoying yourselves. It's great that you are having this excitement, but you are made in the image of God, remember, and you don't want to spoil this. Some of the things you have been told are just not true. The Dutch will not be coming back. I know, because I am Dutch. My whole family is in Holland. I have contacts—my father, my brothers. If the Dutch were coming back, my family would have told me. They are not coming back. You are being fooled. You cannot take over the government jobs because you haven't had enough training. Those of you who want to follow after truth, stay away from these leaders. They are lying to you."

Then the leader stood. "You've heard what our father told us, but he doesn't know everything. Let's get on with it."

From time to time the rebel leader came secretly to John's office, scarely a thousand feet from the government post. Though there was a high price on this man's head, he trusted John. "We want only freedom; we want only better things for our people, better jobs, lower prices. It's time we had a chance to run our own country."

"But this is not the way to get it," John tried to persuade him. John had learned that the movement was connected with the "liberation" front in Papua and had backing from abroad.

As the movement picked up, John went by plane or helicopter to attend the meetings of the rebels. They were getting larger. Again he saw that some of the leaders were professing Christians, using Christian terminology. Many, he felt, sincerely wanted to do what was best for their country.

"Do you want to say a few words?" a leader asked John. John knew that they respected him as their spiritual father, and he felt that he had to warn them because they had been misguided. Many of the Christian leaders took his warning, while in other areas they had been sucked into the movement.

Meanwhile, the rebel movement continued to escalate. John sensed a big demonstration might be in the offing. The rebels had told John that the elections, set for May 1, would never happen. He moved the Bible school graduation and closing, originally set for mid-May, forward to the last week in April. Following graduation on Monday, the students packed up and left for their homes. When on Wednesday it was rumored the rebels were coming to Karubaga, the Dani women and children fled across the mountains.

In his office behind the house, John watched and waited. About 4 P.M., quietly, from every direction, 800 rebels rushed onto the plateau, many of them covered with pig grease and with tusks through their noses. They headed for the airstrip where they ripped up fences and threw them onto the strip. They rolled fuel drums and big rocks out with them. Then they heaped up brush, poles, tree trunks—debris of all kinds until the 2,600-foot strip was covered. The rebels, joined by some of the local Dani men, worked quietly.

The terrified Indonesian government personnel gathered up their families and dashed to the Dekkers' mission house for sanctuary. As two families and four single men surged in, Helen saw a fifth man running down the path with rebels close behind. When she again opened the door, he ran right upstairs to the attic and hid there while Helen slammed the door on the pursuers. The Indonesian officials were so frightened they would not let the children out of their arms.

As darkness came, all was quiet. The next morning when John heard a plane, he thought it must be a reconnaissance flight. Then, as the engines cut, he hurried out to see a commercial plane coming in for a landing. The cloud cover was heavy, and by the time the pilot saw the debris on the strip it was too late to lift up. Though the plane plowed right into the debris, ripping up the wings, the pilot was not injured. He was delivering rice for the election.

"You men have done it now," Dekker called to the Danis who were standing around watching. "Let's get this plane off the runway before something explodes." Somewhat subdued, the rebels pitched in and pulled the plane away from the oil drums. Then John went to the rebel leaders. "You've wrecked this plane which belongs to the Dutch. You said the Dutch are coming back. Well, the people in Holland will hear that because of you they've lost their plane and they won't be happy. But now we must get the women and children out before there is retribution."

"We'll let your mission personnel go, but not the Indonesians," the rebels retorted. John could not sway them. He would have to tell the Indonesians that they could not leave.

"Nobody must get killed," John reminded them. "There must be no bloodshed. It would just lead to more and more killing."

While this negotiating was taking place at the airstrip ten minutes from the Dekkers' house, a new wave of rebels had swept into Karubaga, ransacking the Indonesian houses and government offices, smashing everything in sight. Then they had moved into the Dekkers' yard and were dancing around the house, waving their spears, chanting, and surging forward and back, outside the front window.

They are going to come in here and kill all these people right in this living room, Helen thought as she watched. Yet she was totally calm. When one of the local Dani men summoned her to open the door, she did. "They want your radio," he told Helen.

"I have no radio. Go away."

"Give them your tape recorder," the man replied.

"Why should I? I told you, I have no radio."

"Give them your cassette player."

"No." Helen was adamant. "I said I have no radio. Look at what they're doing to my flower bed!"

The man she was talking to scolded the prancing Danis. "Look what you are doing to Tolibaga's flowers!" The Danis stopped their war dancing and backed off. Helen felt badly later when she discovered that one of the Indonesians had, in fact, brought a radio from his office and hidden it in her attic. "And you let me tell the Danis we didn't have a radio! You made a liar out of me! How could you!"

Later when the rebels returned, Helen got word to John: "I can't hold them off much longer." John hurried up to the house and walked up to the whooping warriors. "Move off, men. My wife is tired of this. As long as these people are in my home they are safe."

As the rebels started to move away, one remained, dancing up and down. Angered, John grabbed the rebel's spear and broke it over his knee, then pounded him with his fists. The startled warrior turned and ran, while John watched, regretting that he had attacked a Dani.

On Friday morning the helicopter was to come in to airlift the mission personnel. "How will we know the helicopter is yours and not from the government?" the rebel chief demanded.

"I'll have him circle three times and land near the hospital," John promised.

Friday morning John was at the helipad with the rebels. The chopper came in, straight down. "I told you to circle," John was yelling. The Danis were standing all around with their spears poised.

"No, no, he's ours!" John called as he rushed onto the helipad, crouching as the chopper settled down. "Wait until you see who gets out!" he yelled to the Danis.

The rebels held their spears tense.

"You see, only the pilot, no military," John insisted. They relaxed while the mission personnel went aboard. Dekker stayed, as did Dr. Wally Donaldson, "just in case someone gets hurt."

Helen was glad to leave. Theo was graduating from eighth grade at the coast—an occasion she didn't want to miss. "John will get through it. He's too tough to die," she tried to convince herself.

Saturday was quiet in Karubaga. As a government helicopter flew over, John yelled at the rebels, "Get down! We don't want anybody to get shot." Again there was no bloodshed.

Sunday also was quiet. The rebels had gone to church. "Let's clear the airstrip," John suggested to Donaldson. As they got to work, a couple of Danis appeared and started to help. Soon there were thirty of them heaving debris out of the way. Soon one third of the strip was cleared. John got on the radio to the MAF: "Send your planes in here. Also planes from RBMU and SIL. I need five, one after another, to get the Indonesian personnel out of here."

So the planes shuttled in and evacuated the Indonesians right in front of a few rebels who were too astonished to lift a finger. Like pulling the teeth of a tiger, this broke the whole rebellion. The elections were held the next day as scheduled.

Because a few rebels still kept sneaking into the area, the Danis patrolled night and day to protect the women and children. Finally John said, "You can't keep this up and you shouldn't leave it to the government to chase these rebels away. You should do it."

For the first time in fifteen years the Christian men took up bows and arrows and chased the rebels out of the district. No one was killed, apart from two men from other areas who were thought to be part of the rebellion and were shot by the military. This was little compared with the bloodbath that occurred in some places where church leaders who had not been clearly directed by mission personnel were deceived and became involved in the rebellion. Hundreds were killed in those areas.

Though church leaders in the area had not become involved in the rebellion, the difficult years between 1977 and
1980 took a toll. The men comprising a military platoon sta-
tioned at Karubaga were not Christians, and they became involved in immorality. Non-Christian Danis who had become
government officials backed the immorality and became involved themselves. The local government head did not punish
them because he too had participated. As a result, uncommit-
ted young people followed suit, and even a few church leaders.
As most of the church leaders preached against the wrongs,
they were beat up. Many injustices took place. Some in the
government wanted to bring back the multiple pig payments
for bride prices and other old practices. The Christians
sometime felt that the forces of Satan were marshaled against
them.

In some ways the rebellion had a positive effect on the
church. Following John's example, leaders had taken a stand
against it, and when it was over they were able to use the
episode as an illustration of how Satan deceives God's people to
draw them away from the truth. Yet, at the same time, the
elders were aware of a growing coldness in the churches of the
Toli Valley.

In June 1980 the three councils invited John to meet
with them to draw up plans for seven evangelistic teams to
campaign in the seventy-nine district churches.

"I suggest, my brothers, that we bring in a man who
has been used of God in evangelism in other areas."

"We can handle this ourselves. Besides, we don't have
the funds to fly anyone in."

"If it doesn't cost anything, would you go along?" John
asked.

They agreed, but not very enthusiastically. He had in
mind Johannes Tabo, an outstanding evangelist from the
C & MA-related churches of the Ilaga. John worked to get the
funding together.

In August John ministered to the teams for three days, reminding them of their basic message and their goals, challenging them to search their own hearts to be sure nothing would hinder the Spirit of God's working through them. After they prayed together the teams fanned out, spending three days in each village. Johannes traveled with them, ministering to the team members and preaching in the villages too. The seventh day they all rested.

For four weeks, they preached, prayed, and challenged. In response, God poured out tremendous blessings on the Toli Valley. Hundreds made decisions to follow Christ. Christians whose hearts had grown cold were revived. The church gave Tabo a great love offering of money, chickens, pigs, and shirts.

The believers began to get up early each morning, bathing in the cold mountain streams before gathering for prayer in the church at five o'clock while it was still dark.

In Wuninip's church at Kanggime about 200 were inside praying when the building began to shake. Thinking it was an earthquake, some jumped from the windows.

"Why are you jumping from the windows?" an overflow crowd outside asked.

"It's an earthquake! Didn't you feel it?" People continued to surge from the church.

"No! No!" the onlookers responded. "We saw the church shake, but the ground did not move. Only the church moved."

"Then it was not an earthquake!" Surprised—and awed —they prayed, "Thank you, God, for this sign of your power."

Wuninip had been encouraged by the number of people meeting for prayer in the mornings. Now he reflected on the fresh reminder that the One to whom they prayed each morning was all-powerful.

While wonderful healings had occurred since the earliest days of the Dani church, they were more frequent during the revival. Although not all healings were clinically confirmed, they greatly encouraged the faith of the Dani believers. The Christians took advantage of medical help, but knew that ultimately they could depend only on God.

In the Karubaga church, Ogogu had not responded to medical treatment. His stomach became large and distended. In early 1983 he called for the local pastor, Musa, and the elders to pray for him. Immediately he had relief, and over the next few weeks he was completely healed.

. A woman by the name of Ninggen in the village of Kowari suddenly became very ill, first foaming at the mouth and then losing consciousness. The people had prepared the wood for her funeral pyre. "She is *kanggerak* (she has died)," they said.

Jan Yikwa, a teacher at the Dani Bible school, was visiting the village. After he and others prayed for her, Jan advised the relatives to take her to the clinic. On the way she revived. Her father was so happy that he wanted to give Jan a leg of pork. But Jan said, "No, it was not my work, but God's."

Butiman and Laale had sought all the medical help available, but were given up for dead. Friends had gathered to pay their last respects; the funeral pyre was waiting. Musa, the local pastor, was called in as a last resort. As he and the elders prayed, the Lord responded by dramatically healing the two. These were tremendous testimonies to the Lord's power. People realized God had worked miracles on their behalf through the prayers of the church.

Many children, too, were prayed for when parents had despaired of their lives. In June 1983 little Kina's father broke down and cried, fearing she would die. Medicine had failed. Jan, who was visiting the village, urged the man to have faith. "I'll get some of the students from the school, and we'll be back to pray for her." He and the students formed a circle around the girl and asked the Lord to raise her up. Soon the little girl sat up, took a drink of water, and then ate. The next day she was in school.

Amberingga had always opposed the gospel. The opposition increased to the point where the Christians wondered if he was possessed. "Why don't we pray especially for this man?" an elder suggested. After all the elders had joined in prayer for the man, they gathered around him. "O Lord, we ask you by your power to dispel whatever possesses Amber- ingga and set him free so he can become one of your children. We ask this in Jesus' name." As they prayed, "something like a butterfly came out of him," and immediately the man was in his right mind. Quietly he sat down to listen to the gospel. Amberingga testified to all around about what God had done for him. "Now I want to learn God's Word," he told the elders.

The people of Kanggime knew Ndaganiyapmban Lambe had been a very sick man for many years. Medical workers had sent him to the hospital in Mulia, but there was no improvement until one day a visitor was reading to him from the Bible.

"Is any sick among you? Let him call for the elders of the church, and let them pray over him, anointing him with oil in the name of the Lord; and the prayer of faith shall save the sick, and the Lord shall raise him up" (James 5:14, 15, KJV).

"Where are you reading, my brother?" the sick man asked.

"From the Book of James."

"These words—they are for us too, are they not?"

"Yes, I believe that."

"Then I would like the elders to pray for me and to anoint me."

The elders came and gathered around the man's bed. With expectation, the sick man and the elders joined their hearts in asking God for healing.

Then there was rejoicing and thanksgiving.

"If we added the healings in the churches in other areas with those in Karubaga and Kanggime, there would be hun- dreds of cases where the Lord has miraculously intervened on behalf of his people," Jan Yikwa declared.

And all was under the sovereign moving of God; RBMU mission personnel had not promoted it in any way.

16 Courage

While Pubu was teaching the Bible in his Toli Valley village and was looking forward to attending Maranatha Bible School, he heard that there were Yalis who ate people. The thought that men made in the image of God would eat their fellowman so upset Pubu that he decided to go directly to those Yalis. *They need to hear about God and his way of salvation.*

Pubu arrived in Ninia, intending to go on to Yalisili, a day's trek south. "It is hard to grow potatoes in that area. And it is far too dangerous," he was warned. Others reminded him that two Yali evangelists had been killed and the Western missionary Stan Dale seriously wounded there.

"Should I stay here in Ninia, or should I go to Yalisili?" Pubu prayed that night. "You have called me here to do your work. Please show me now what I should do."

His answer came in a vivid dream in which he saw himself with his daughter Yebit on his shoulder and his wife Mbeli behind him on the trail to Yalisili.

As Pubu and Mbeli trekked the rugged trail, heavy clouds settled into an unbroken ceiling above them. "We will not get to the first village before the rain begins will we, Pubu?"

Pubu had looked up a dozen times, but he did so again to delay telling Mbeli that they would not beat the rain, even by stepping up their pace which they had already done. When the hard rain came, they had to slow down to keep from losing their footing on the steep, muddy trail. On Pubu's shoulders, Yebit whimpered and snuggled her face against Pubu's head in search of any protection it might offer.

In the first village on the trail between Ninia and Yalisili, the residents had taken shelter from the downpour. In one of the huts a man sat near the door, watching the rain soak his sweet potato garden and at the same time thinking about his uncle who had recently died. His daydreams were interrupted by movement on the village path. Then through the blur of rain he saw a face that reminded him of his late uncle. Forgetting about the rain, he ran out, loudly exclaiming, "My uncle's spirit has come to visit us!" Out of the huts others came for the reunion.

"No, no!" Pubu protested, "I am not a spirit! I am a man. I have come to tell you how to be saved from the place of fire and flames, and to tell you about Jesus and what he has done for me."

In spite of any disappointment the villagers might have felt that it wasn't the departed uncle's spirit, they allowed the rain-bedraggled strangers to spend the night in the village. The next day Pubu and his family went on to Yalisili, where their reception was friendly. An older man invited them to stay with him in his house. Soon afterward village leaders gave their permission to Pubu to build a house. He was even more surprised when they helped. It was completed in one day.

Learning the language wasn't as easy as building the house. At first Pubu was tempted to return home, but in response to his prayer the Lord helped him to learn the Yali language quickly. In fact, he became the best of all the Danis in speaking the Yali language.

As some showed interest in the gospel, they built a simple church of poles and pandanus leaves. The next year, when RBMU began work on a landing strip at Holuwon, about an hour's walk from Yalisili, Pubu went to help. In his absence some of the Yalisili people made new fetishes. Nobody went to church or cared when the goats moved into it, and the roof leaked. When Pubu heard this, he went to Yalisili and scolded the people. "You think you're religious because you have a church building, but it means nothing if you're not there to worship God and learn of him. You think you're Christians, but you don't want to listen to God's Word. If you want to return to witchcraft and let the goats mess up the church, I'm going to burn it down!" With that announcement he threw kerosene on the building and put a match to it.

"Jesus said to shake the dust off your feet wherever people won't receive the gospel," Pubu said. As he returned to Holuwon the people wailed, "*Ayee*—he burned our church down! *Ayee*! All that work!"

While the church burned, a young Christian who had gone to Holuwon with Pubu and had come home with him discovered his house had been taken over by the chief. In anger he took a flaming brand and torched the house where the chief was living. It quickly went up in flames, destroying the chief's clothes, axe, and bush knife. The incensed Yali got all the warriors together. "We'll kill Pubu," they decided. "If the Holuwon people want to protect him, we'll chase them all from the plateau." Throughout the night they sent messages to the surrounding villages: "Come and help us." Midmorning they headed for Holuwon.

In Holuwon Pubu, unaware that the chief's house in Yalisili had been torched, wondered what the sudden cries of the villagers meant. Then he heard, "Pubu, Pubu! Yalisli warriors are coming!" By then they were close enough for Pubu to see the paint on their faces and the pig tusks through their noses.

"Mbeli, children, quick—run to the Wilsons' house!"

John Wilson and his wife had arrived shortly before, and already the new missionaries had a wanted Dani in their midst. Outside, the Yali warriors danced and crowded around the house, calling, "Come out, Pubu. We're going to kill you!"

"Don't go out, Pubu." John held him back. But Pubu pushed past him and stepped outside, closing the door behind him. He stood before the angry mob and calmly challenged, "Go ahead, kill me. I am not afraid. God sent me to give you his message, and if you now want to kill me, do it."

The taunts and the dancing stopped. Then they turned and surged toward Pubu's house, ripping it down and tearing up his garden.

By this time Lelai, the Holuwon chief, was furious. "They are killing our teacher!" he cried. At this, all the Christian young men from the village joined in the battle, swinging clubs, snatching bows and arrows and breaking them, and chasing the invaders from the area. Nobody was killed, but many got bloody heads, and some got arrows in their bodies.

One of the RBMU missionaries rebuked Pubu for burning the church and recommended that he should make restitution. Pubu paid a pig. Later the people decided that Pubu had been a good teacher, and they called him back to Yalisili to minister again. They built a new church which was better than the one he had torched. They also built him a better house, and he came to live with them once more.

A day's journey south in Uwam, the village leaders had gathered at Belak's request.

"I've heard things are different in Ninia and Yalisili since the Danis came with their *kiwone*, as they call it. Many don't want to fight anymore. They listen to a Pubu and others speak about God and—"

"What are you saying, Belak?" a younger Yali curtly interrupted.

"I am saying that we should invite this Pubu to Uwam to hear this gospel ourselves. You see, when I was younger I heard an old man prophesy that 'new words would come to replace the old.'"

"You think this Dani has the new words?" the young Yali asked with a bit of a smirk.

"I feel that this may be so," Belak replied.

"Yes, Belak, let's invite this man here to speak to us," another leader agreed.

All were curious, if not convinced.

When Pubu arrived to speak, Belak had the people organized for a fetish burning. "No, wait. You must understand what you are doing," Pubu admonished. Then as Pubu preached the gospel, many listened and accepted it. As Belak grew in the Lord, he began taking a group of men and trekking down to the lowlands. There he made the first contact with the Somahai people, telling them, "When I saw what the gospel had done for us, I felt we had to take it to you." From there the gospel spread to Sumo, which became a base for mission outreach.

Kileloho also came to the Lord through Pubu and went as a manual worker to Sumo. Later he attended Maranatha Bible School and graduated. He and his wife, Filiren, an earnest couple, went to the Sumahai tribe. Elabo, another convert of Pubu's ministry, emerged as a strong spiritual leader in the Holuwon area and attended Bible school also.

Pubu watched young men who had turned to God through his ministry leave for Bible school in Karubaga. He recalled how in his urgency to go to the cannibalistic Yalis he had not attended Bible school as he had planned. It was not too late, he decided. He needed more training. "It is time for me to go school too," he announced.

In a personal evangelism class the teacher asked Elabo, "How did you become a Christian?" Elabo turned around and pointed to Pubu: "That man led me to the Lord." Elabo became a respected minister to many up and down the valley, a man with deep personal concern for all, and a good leader.

Later Pubu went back to Yalisili for a month to encourage them. They looked upon him as their spiritual father; yet there was a certain coldness and indifference. "Perhaps if the missionaries had stuck by Pubu at the time of the church burning, the people might be more responsive today," a leading Yali pastor suggests.

Tarin had already planted a church among the Kimyal people of the eastern highlands, but felt God's call to venture into a new area, far to the south of Sumo in the lowlands. After taking a furlough among his own people in the Toli Valley he set out, going first without his family and with another Dani missionary, Nggiwunggen. They made a potato garden to insure having food when their families came. After the men stayed a few months attempting to learn the difficult language, they returned in January 1981 for Tarin's wife and three younger children. The oldest three stayed behind to attend school.

Soon after the family's arrival in the lowlands, four-year-old Bayita fell on a slippery log, injuring her head and back on a fallen tree. The following day she died. The heartbroken parents prayed, "Our Father, we have not come to this area for our own good, but because you called us here. You must be in control of the situation. We will trust you." They buried their child right there and worked to open up the difficult area.

Then Tarin's wife Yabok and a son, Wayon, began to have trouble with their feet swelling so badly they could not walk. "It is the dreaded *filariases*. You will certainly die of this," the people gloomily predicted.

"Tarin, I want to go to the doctor," Yabok pleaded. But they were in an isolated area, and the landing strip was not yet ready.

"My wife, perhaps we should not go immediately to the

doctor. Let us first pray to the Lord, and ask him to heal you and our son. Because the people here cannot go to the doctor every time they are sick, we must show them that we have a doctor in the Lord himself—that he can heal our sicknesses.

"Lord, we have come here to serve you. We have lost one child, and now two of us are sick. We know you can heal and strengthen, and we commit ourselves to you. We believe it is the enemy that is causing this sickness. He does not want us bringing the word of God to these Dekai people. We take a stand against the enemy. And we ask you to heal the feet of Yabok and Wayon."

In a short time both were up and walking again. As a result their faith was strengthened and they rejoiced that the Lord had called them to this place. "Even though we have lost our daughter, it is a privilege to pioneer this new area for Jesus Christ." They praised God through their tears.

The people had been watching to see how Tarin's family would react to the death of their child. Now as they saw how the Lord healed the feet of Tarin's wife and son, they admitted, "Some of our people have had this same problem, but they died. Your God has healed in answer to your prayers!" they exclaimed.

"Tarin and Yabok, you said you had come to bring us good news, and we can see that it is good news to have a God who is so powerful in the face of the diseases and troubles you have been passing through."

Tarin thought about that. He didn't want them turning to God just to save them from trouble. He taught them, "If we live, we live to the Lord; and if we die, we die to the Lord. So that whether we live or die, we belong to the Lord" (Romans 14:8, NIV). The people listened intently, knowing he was talking from his heart, out of the depths of his own experience. This made a great impression on them, and many responded.

"Tarin, in the past we have thought just of ourselves and not of the Lord. Now you have shown us that we belong to

God regardless of what comes into our lives. We want you to stay with us and teach us more words from God."

Wiyarenit and his wife Wanagarak volunteered to pioneer in an isolated village many hours' trekking distance beyond the station of Suntamon into the farthest eastern highlands. Their two oldest children were left behind at school, and four went with them. The helicopter dropped them on the high mountain plateau in a place called Mbonggok. The people there gave Wiyarenit space, and he immediately set about making his sweet potato garden. About three months later, before the garden had begun to produce, the family ran out of food. The mission had sent in rice by helicopter, but it was gone. For several days clouds had shut them in so that no further drop was possible. The people who lived there would not share out of their meager food supply. As a result the children of the missionaries were very hungry for sweet potatoes, especially Arekap and Yorit.

A thought had been taking root in Arekap's mind. "There is always food at Suntamon. I'll walk there, and maybe they will have sweet potatoes. I'll take Yorit with me." Arekap was sure she knew how to get there, but at thirteen she failed to consider the great distance involved. It was already two in the afternoon when she and Yorit left. At four they were still ascending the mountain when a heavy rain slowed them. Yorit began to cry. "I'll carry you," the big sister comforted him as she put him on her shoulder. On and on she trudged, feeling the weight of her six-year-old brother. Finally they went through the pass and started down the other side, which was muddy as well as steep.

When they reached the river, it was already dusk. The stepping-stones in the river were slippery and the water around them so swift that Arekap stopped short of crossing. "I can't carry you across the river here, Yorit. I'm afraid I'll slip." He was too young to try it himself, she decided. They searched along the shore for a better place to cross, but by then it was so dark she couldn't see stones if they were there. Feeling more hungry and frightened, she went back up to the pass, to a sheltered place she had noticed on the way down. "We'll spend the night here, Yorit." She tried to hide her fear, but they were both so chilled from being wet that they could hardly feel their hands and feet. Crying and frightened, they crawled under boughs and leaves behind the crag in the mountain. The rain came right through, soaking them as they huddled together in despair, shivering in the bitter cold of the 5,000-foot altitude. Despite her hunger, Arekap would have given anything to be home. *Oh why—why did I—* "Yorit, Yorit!" He was still. Then Arekap lost consciousness.

"Where are the children?" Wiyarenit had asked when he came home that evening. "I thought they were with you," Wanagarak replied. Checking with the villagers, they were told the children had gone with one of the men over to Suntamon. The parents were sure their children were all right.

Later that night Wanagarak wakened. "The spirit of Yorit has come to me. The children have died!"

Immediately Wiyarenit set out on the trail. He ran up the mountain through the pass and right past the place where the children huddled just off the trail; but because it was dark he did not see them. He hurried down the mountain and across the river. Reaching Suntamon at dawn, he went to the Dani missionary house. "Have you seen my children?" he asked. Anxiety was on his face and in his voice.

"No, they have not been here," the missionary reluctantly told him. They knew that something was very wrong, and together they set out back over the mountain.

The older man whom the villagers thought had taken the children with him had spent the night in the pass. In the morning he started down the trail, and as he came to the little shelter where Arekap and Yorit huddled during the long bitter night, he heard crying.

"Arekap!" Then he saw the dead boy. "Come, I'll take you to Suntamon."

As they approached the river, they met the children's father as he was returning to search for them. "Wiyarenit, Yorit is—" Wiyarenit didn't hear the last word. Arekap was sobbing. "We were going to get potatoes—" The girl could say no more.

Wiyarenit raced up to the pass and found the body of his little boy. As he held the dead child in his arms, he cried through his tears, "O God, I have come to this place because you called me. Now you have taken my son to your house. This is very sad for me, but I know you can bring good out of it." Carefully, through his tears, Wiyarenit carried his child's body to the mission station at Suntamon and sent a runner back with word to Wanagarak, who traveled through the night over the treacherous trail, arriving at daybreak in Suntamon.

The sad couple decided that they would not follow the Dani custom of cremation, but would bury the body of this beloved son. Seeing their sorrow, the Christians felt deeply for the grieving parents and donated towels and a blanket to wrap the body. Then they buried Yorit.

A week later John and Helen came to the village of Suntamon as part of their Dani missionary tour. Wiyarenit and Wanagarak poured out their loss, as well as the struggles and disappointments of the pioneer field in the brief time they had been there. Helen sat in the hut on a misty hillside, arms around Wanagarak, as they cried together over little Yorit's death. Outside, John and Wiyarenit stood looking at the cluster of huts on the narrow plateau.

"It's been so hard." Wiyarenit's face and voice confirmed that. "The language is difficult. There is so little sunshine that our sweet potatoes take much longer to grow. These people do not really want us. They do not share their food with us, even when our children are hungry. That's why our Yorit is dead." And he told John the story.

"This week we have been tempted to go home," he admitted. "Will these people ever believe? Will we ever have a church?"

"Yes," John assured him, "These people have been made in the image of God just like you and me. The same grace of God reaches out to them as it did to us. The same wonderful love can work in their hearts."

"Yes, that is true. In the old days our hearts were like stone, but since the Holy Spirit has come into our hearts we have learned to love. We must show it."

The people of Mbongok realized the sincere love Wiyarenit had for them, even in the midst of his sorrow. Soon afterward some were baptized. A church came into being.

As the church became strong, a number of its leaders, along with Wiyarenit, began treks to people in faraway valleys, to take them the gospel of Christ they had come to love with all their hearts.

John mused on his Dani colleague's words as the Missionary Aviation Fellowship helicopter carried Helen and him between the jagged ridges and over hills to the next missionary couple they were to visit.

"We have learned to love," Wiyarenit had said. That's something I've had to learn too, and still have to learn. He looked at Helen whose face, pressed to the window, eagerly searched the dense green forest below for any new cluster of round thatched roofs, indicating another village yet to hear the transforming gospel of Jesus Christ. As John reached across and squeezed her hand, she turned to smile at him. Then, competing with the noise of the chopper, John shouted, "Hi, doll! You're such a little hero. I still love you."

Tears flooded Helen's eyes, and John searched his heart. *What did I know of love when I asked Helen to marry me? I only knew she was the helpmate God was giving me for missionary service.*

17 New Independence

John and Helen continued to visit the seventy-nine Toli Valley churches and the sixty-five Dani missionary couples. Just as John had kept his eyes open for culture shock when he served as field chairman among RBMU missionaries, he looked for signs among the Dani missionaries. For both groups they were the same: overidentification with the people they had come to reach—eating what they eat, dressing (or undressing) as they did, or the more common tendency to isolate themselves in their own comfort zone, away from the dirt and distressing customs surrounding them.

At the Dani missions John sometimes was asked to preach, but usually he listened. "We come, and we go. But you have God's Word in your hands, and it will stay. That is what is important," he told them.

Occasionally he was startled by the illustrations that accompanied the Danis' teaching. "The Holy Spirit is like a dog," a Dani missionary said with gusto. John listened intently as the analogy developed. "When the Dani people go into the forest to hunt for possum and other animals, they take their dogs along. Without a dog it would be hopeless to spot the animals, but the dog smells them out and gives the hunter a chance to shoot them. That's the way the Holy Spirit convicts the Christian of sin and gives him a chance to put it out of his life," the Dani explained.

"Not a bad illustration after all," John conceded.

He was concerned that so few Danis were setting aside a regular time each day for reading God's Word and praying. In his visits he stressed the need for this. It was a difficult discipline, because their culture was oriented to doing things as they felt like it. Many of the Christian leaders listened to John's instruction and developed a daily study time.

He found the inevitable problems and differences that accompany any effort by a group of people, especially with varied cultural backgrounds. The Yalis and the people of the south coast sometimes felt that the Danis were too paternalistic. "He wants to be the big chief all the time" or "He does all the baptizing. Why doesn't he give us a chance?" they complained.

In some places the Danis insisted that the people order their services in the same way the Danis did. "It is the Christian way," they said. In some places they insisted that the Christian songs be sung in the Dani way, tried to clothe their converts in the Dani attire, and tended to stay too long rather than turning the work over to the local church leaders and moving on to new fields. Such problems were isolated. More often John found the Danis have been able to adjust and have passed on the leadership to local Christians. In Ninia, where there were at one time twenty Dani couples, the work is totally in Yali hands.

In some instances there have been misunderstandings about the roles and responsibilities of the Danis and the Western missionaries. Not all Westerners have been able to fit into a helping role, especially when a young Western missionary joins a Dani missionary who has been in the place for several years, has opened up the work, and planted a fledgling church. Perhaps the new man finds it difficult to appreciate the Dani's efforts and is upset when the senior Dani does not accept his suggestions. He sees the people reciting the Scriptures together as too mechanical to be of any benefit, or criticizes the work projects the Dani has the people involved in as inappropriate. He sees the Dani as too bossy and authoritarian. The Dani missionary is disappointed that his Western colleague does not give him the help he expected, and a conflict develops. Sometimes it is a personality clash.

"Generally, though, there has been excellent working together, with each acknowledging what the other brings," John observed. The Danis appreciate the things that go along with the Western presence—the aircraft, radios, medicines, and translation skills—all needed in missionary outreach. They recognize that they don't have these.

When Helen was able to go along on these trips, she sat with the Dani missionary wives while they poured out their loneliness. Usually the Dani missionaries were alone at their post, a day's walk or so beyond the mission base, and often without a radio. The wives were frustrated and concerned when there wasn't enough food for their families. In areas where the people were hostile and unclean, the Dani women longed to be back in their clean villages in the Toli Valley, among their loved ones.

"These people are so mean and indifferent. They don't care about God's Word. They don't care what happens to us —even when my baby got sick and died," the Dani woman cried as she told about it.

"Do you remember when I first came among you?" Helen asked them. "I had my precious little babies, and you all seemed so dirty. You didn't seem to want us. And you didn't seem to want the Lord. I sat and cried. Over and over, 'my heart left me.' But God gave me grace, and I stayed. I, too, had to send my children away to school," she reminded them. "He'll give you grace so that you can stay in these difficult places and bear separation from loved ones."

"We didn't know you had these problems," the Dani

woman replied, and they cried together, thankful for someone who understood.

John looked out on the late afternoon mist which characterized Kanggime. He reflected on the Dani church—its growth and the obvious blessings of God on it. "The Place Where I Die" had found new life. With it had come hope instead of despair, love instead of hate. Acting on new attributes, its people had shared the Source of their new life with neighbors and with faraway tribes on this Pacific island. Increasingly John's mind had been on places where this was not so. As during that ride across the Canadian prairies many years before, a new awareness of those who had not heard the gospel was disrupting his status quo. Was it time for him to move on? If God was leading him out of Irian Jaya, he needed to confirm it. One way would be to get Wuninip's perspective on the Toli Valley churches and John's role in relation to them. He would see Wuninip soon.

"Wuninip, if I were to stay here, what would you want me to do?" John asked.

"Tolibaga, you have been our father for these many years and we want you to stay with us, to advise as necessary, to help with the distribution and supply of medicines, to order the trade goods and arrange the flights, and to supervise the community development." And then he added, "Now that the Bible school is almost nationalized, your regular teaching of the church leaders really won't be necessary."

John found this very interesting. He had been with the Dani church from the beginning and had often felt it was too dependent on him. It was different now. Earlier only parts of the New Testament had been available, but now the entire New Testament was translated and in book form. A competent missionary force in the Toli area worked along with the Dani church, giving assistance in the Bible school, the medical work, the youth and women's work, and various community development projects when needed. Max and Bev Winch from Australia had joined the missionary force to work among the Danis in the Mamit area. *Max is well-fitted to take over my role.*

He thought of the Dani Christian leaders emerging, young men like Timothy Wakur who had studied at the Evangelical Institute of Indonesia and was recently appointed principal of the Indonesian Maranatha Bible School at Karubaga.

In all of this and in the words of Isaiah God seemed to be telling him, "Enlarge the place of your tent, stretch your tent curtains wide. Do not hold back" (Isaiah 54:2, NIV). But where? How? When?

In June 1981 after twenty-one years in Irian Jaya, John and Helen gathered up their things and said good-bye to the Dani church. As John was leaving Kanggime for the last time, old Nigitbaga hobbled over to see him off. "Tolibaga, do you remember when you baptized me and God restored my sight?"

"Sure I do," Dekker replied, hugging the old man who had adopted John's family.

"Tolibaga, I won't see you again in this world, but I will see you in Heaven! Farewell, my father."

As John flew eastward, he thought about the brave band of Danis he left behind—at Kanggime, on the south coast, in the Lakes Plain district and in the highlands. The Danis had penetrated many areas of Irian Jaya in twenty years.

"Thank you, Lord, for the courage of the Danis. Use it for your glory to motivate others to reach the unreached in their countries—and in regions beyond."

Epilogue

The story of Danis reaching out to other tribes in Irian Jaya is an example that John Dekker hopes nationals will copy in their own land. It is a plan of action that must be used in every part of the world if unreached peoples are to hear the gospel. How else will we ever get the job done? he asks.

John returned from Irian Jaya with the burden to encourage and stimulate Christian nationals to become involved with outreach to people groups within their own country and in countries beyond. As a member of Christian Nationals Evangelism Commission (CNEC), he challenges and helps Christian nationals in Third-World countries to take on the task—to consider the Dani experience and say, "With God's help, we too can reach out!" To them, his emphasis is the same as it was to the Danis—stewardship, giving of self, and sharing the Good News. From his experience he offers missiological principles which he and other Western missionaries applied in their initial contact with the Danis and which nationals can apply in evangelizing nationals. (See page 193.)

In his travels John hears the excuse, "We are too poor and too uneducated to do missionary work; that is the work of Western churches." From the Bible he points out their responsibility and uses the Dani missionary enterprise as an example of how poor uneducated people did it.

A Liberian evangelist wrote to CNEC that he had seen films of the Dani work at a church conference in Monrovia and that their example had been a powerful model for him. "We are so grateful to you for sending Rev. John Dekker to show us the very educative films of some other poor Christians. We are going back to do what we saw in the pictures."

This is a book about reaching those who have never heard the gospel. Yet, its emphasis on outreach extends also to those who *have heard*. They too are unreached in the ultimate sense until they personally believe.

Missiological Principles

In their mission to the Danis of Irian Jaya, John Dekker and other missionary personnel felt led to practice the following principles, even though all had not been thoroughly tested.

Finances: 1) No foreign funds were used in developing the local churches. 2) The Dani Christians shared the gospel freely throughout the area, and the mission employed no paid evangelists. 3) Missionaries did not burden the Dani Christians with any church structure they could not manage themselves, including payment of pastors. Members of congregations paid pastors by cultivating gardens for them and providing other needs. 4) The principle of self-support was practiced in church and community life. 5) To avoid the development of "rice Christians," no preferential treatment was given to Christians in medical and community development work. 6) Stewardship was taught from the start.

Church government: 1) Leadership of local churches was in the hands of the Dani Christians as soon as a church was established. 2) New Christians were not appointed to leadership positions. 3) Local congregations exercised church discipline, sometimes assisted by the area church council. 4) The local churches chose/affirmed who would attend Bible school. 5) The Dani church was allowed to develop its own structure in the context of Dani society and in agreement with the Scriptures. 6) No outside liturgies or music were introduced in the church service.

Education: 1) Literacy schools were introduced in the first stages of church planting. 2) Christian doctrine (in the form of catechism) was introduced in the early life of the church. 3) Recognizing the distinction between the cultural and supracultural elements of the gospel, contextualization as well as dynamic equivalences were used in presenting the Christian message. 4) Teaching began with what was known to the Denis and moved on to the unknown.

Evangelization: 1) The self-propagating principle was carefully taught, and evangelization of the Toli area was largely done by Dani Christians. 2) Dani missionary outreach became an important part of the church early in its development. 3) The webbing principle (spreading the gospel through contacts with family, friends, business people, etc.) was very much a part of the rapid church growth.

The Dekkers
Today

"We wouldn't trade our missionary experience for anything in the world," the Dekker children agree today. They always dreaded good-byes, and the separations during boarding school days were difficult. Yet, they remember the family times at the coast as happy ones. Paul went on to LeTourneau College and Eva to Wheaton. Theo is currently studying at Evangel, and Dan is at Pasadena City College. Paul married Wendy Evans, and Theo married Lee Ann Eby—both "MKs" and high school sweethearts from Ukarumpa in Papua New Guinea. Eva's husband is Steve Long, whom she met at Wheaton. They have a daughter, Cherith. All are seeking to serve the Lord wholeheartedly.

Helen says, "We went to a place called 'Evil Spirit' or 'The Place Where I Die.' It became this for me. Jesus allowed me to be crushed, to agonize, to die to all that I held precious. The enemy's heavy attacks made deep inroads in our marriage and our health, but I wouldn't exchange a day of it. For God, by his grace and faithfulness, kept me there.

"Most outstanding were the times of mighty outpourings of the Holy Spirit, revealing Jesus as a very close burden-bearer. His comfort allowed new beginnings so that I could serve him with eagerness and joy.

"God has wonderfully enriched our marriage and our childrens' lives. He is a wonderful and wise God!"

While most of John's time today is devoted to encouraging and challenging national brethren throughout the world to share the gospel with people groups within their own countries who as yet have never heard the Good News, he is also available to speak in churches and to participate in missionary conferences. Prayer support for this strategic ministry is needed and appreciated.

Ethnographic, church growth, and mission films taken by John Dekker in Irian Jaya are available through Christian Nationals Evangelism Commission, 1470 North Fourth Street, P.O. Box 15025, San Jose, CA 95115-0025; phone (408) 298-0965.

Notes

Chapter 3 Unlikely Pair

1. Now RBMU International.
2. The UFM had two branches involved, the North American and Australian, which later became known as the Asian Pacific Christian Mission (APCM). See Shirley Horne, *An Hour to the Stone Age* (Chicago: Moody Press, 1973).
3. See Russell Hitt, *Cannibal Valley* (Harrisburg, Penn.: Christian Publications, 1981).
4. Author of *Peace Child* (Glendale, Calif.: Regal, 1974).

Chapter 5 The Neighbors

1. C & MA missionary Gordon Larson brought Ilago believers to witness to other Danis in several regions. See Alice Gibbons, *The People Time Forgot* (Chicago: Moody Press, 1981).

Chapter 6 Kiwone

1. See *ibid.*

Chapter 7 "O Creator, Greetings"

1. From the story of the Good Samaritan (Luke 10:25–37).

Chapter 8 Breakthroughs

1. See Don Richardson, *Lords of the Earth* (Glendale, Calif.: Regal, 1974).

Chapter 9 Change

1. Meaning unknown.

Chapter 11 A Growing Church

1. While such cases were not clinically confirmed and comatose conditions may have existed, these incidents strengthened the faith of the people.

Chapter 12 Bold Moves

1. The setting for *Peace Child* was twenty-four miles northwest of Kawem.

Chapter 13 Reaching Out

1. Indonesian currency. 1000 rupiah equals $1 in U.S. currency. After the Indonesian takeover in 1963, currency replaced cowrie shells.